Emerging Visions for Access in the Twenty-first Century Library

CONFERENCE PROCEEDINGS
DOCUMENTATION ABSTRACTS, INC.
INSTITUTES FOR INFORMATION SCIENCE
APRIL 21–22, 2003

Presented by
the Council on Library and Information Resources
and the California Digital Library

Council on Library and Information Resources

Washington, D.C.

August 2003

Documentation Abstracts, Inc.
Institutes for Information Science

"Emerging Visions for Access in the Twenty-first Century Library" is the second in a series of international symposiums that are supported by a grant from Documentation Abstracts, Inc. (DAI). The institutes will address key issues in information science relating to digital libraries, economics of information, or resources for scholarship.

Documentation Abstracts, Inc., was established in 1966 as a nonprofit organization comprising representatives from eight societies in the field of library and information science: American Chemical Society—Division of Chemical Information, American Library Association, American Society of Indexers, American Society for Information Science and Technology, Association of Information and Dissemination Centers, Association for Library and Information Science Education, Medical Library Association, and Special Libraries Association.

DAI was established to organize, evaluate, and disseminate information and knowledge concerning the various aspects of information science. It did this through publishing Information Science Abstracts (ISA), a bimonthly abstracting and indexing publication covering the literature of information science worldwide. In June 1998, this periodical was acquired by Information Today, Inc., which continues its publication to date.

The California Digital Library (CDL) is the eleventh university library of the University of California. It was established in 1997 to build the university's digital library, help campus libraries share their resources and holdings more effectively, and provide leadership in applying information technology to the development of the university's library collections and services.

Harnessing technology and innovation, and leveraging the intellectual and cultural resources of the University of California, the CDL supports the assembly and creative use of the world's scholarship and knowledge for the University of California libraries and the communities they serve.

The Council on Library and Information Resources (CLIR) is an independent, nonprofit organization that works to expand access to information, however recorded and preserved, as a public good.

CLIR identifies barriers to information access and use, and helps society understand what is at risk in the changing information environment. In partnership with other organizations, CLIR helps create services that expand the concept of "library" and supports the providers and preservers of information. CLIR's agenda is enhanced by the work of the Digital Library Federation (DLF), a consortium of libraries and related agencies that are pioneering the use of electronic information technologies to extend their collections and services. The DLF operates under the umbrella of CLIR.

ISBN 1-932326-03-0

Published by:

Council on Library and Information Resources
1755 Massachusetts Avenue, NW, Suite 500
Washington, DC 20036
Web site at http://www.clir.org

Additional copies are available for $20 per copy. Orders must be placed through CLIR's Web site.

 The paper in this publication meets the minimum requirements of the American National Standard for Information Sciences—Permanence of Paper for Printed Library Materials ANSI Z39.48-1984.

Copyright 2003 by the Council on Library and Information Resources. No part of this publication may be reproduced or transcribed in any form without permission of the publisher. Requests for reproduction should be submitted to the Director of Communications at the Council on Library and Information Resources.

Contents

About the Authors iv

Preface vi

Welcoming Remarks, *Lawrence H. Pitts* 1

Reaching across Library Boundaries, *Robert S. Martin* 3

The Library and Society: Emerging Roles for the Library as a Civic Institution

    The Personal Library: Integrating the Library in the Networking
    Society, *Jens Thorhauge* 17

    Libraries Empower People to Participate in a Civil Society,
    Gary E. Strong 27

    Toward Supported "Communities of Interest" in Digital Environments,
    Robin Stanton 33

The Library and Education: Integrating Information Landscapes,
Michael A. McRobbie 44

New Models for Stewardship

    The Open Access Movement in Scholarly Communication,
    Michael Eisen 56

    Lessons in Deep Resource Sharing from the University of California
    Libraries, *Daniel Greenstein* 66

About the Authors

Michael Eisen is a scientist in the Life Sciences Division, Lawrence Berkeley National Lab, and adjunct assistant professor, Department of Molecular and Cellular Biology, University of California at Berkeley. He is also cofounder of the Public Library of Science, a nonprofit organization of scientists committed to making the world's scientific and medical literature a public resource. It is working to establish online public libraries and science that will archive and freely distribute the complete contents of every published scientific article, greatly expand access to scientific knowledge, facilitate research, and inform medical practice.

Daniel Greenstein is University of California university librarian for system-wide library planning and scholarly information and executive director of the California Digital Library. Before joining the University of California, he was director of the U.S.-based Digital Library Federation and founding director of two networked information services working on behalf of the United Kingdom's universities and colleges.

Robert S. Martin is director of the Institute of Museum and Library Services. Before that appointment in 2001, he was professor and interim director of the School of Library and Information Studies at Texas Woman's University. He has also served as director and librarian of the Texas State Library and Archives Commission and associate dean of libraries for special collections at Louisiana State University. He served as acting chairman of the National Endowment for the Arts from October 2001 through January 2002.

Michael A. McRobbie is vice president for information technology and chief information officer at Indiana University. He is responsible for information technology on all seven campuses of Indiana University. He is also professor of computer science, informatics, and philosophy, as well as adjunct professor of cognitive science and information science on the Bloomington campus. In addition, he is professor of computer technology in the School of Engineering at Indiana University-Purdue University Indianapolis (IUPUI). In July 2003, he assumed the additional title of Indiana University vice president for research. He is also chief executive officer of Pervasive Technology Libraries and chief information architect for the Indiana Genomics Initiative.

Lawrence H. Pitts is vice chair of the Academic Senate of the University of California and a faculty representative to the Regents. He currently is professor of neurosurgery at UC San Francisco and was their Academic Senate chair.

Robin Stanton has been pro vice-chancellor (information) at the Australian National University since 1998. He is responsible for the university's information infrastructure, including scholarly, corporate, and information technology services. From 1993 to 1998, he was the dean of the Faculty of Engineering and Information Technology and, before that, head of Computer Science and director of the Cooperative Research Centre (CRC) in Advanced Computation. He is a Fellow of the Australian Academy of Technological Sciences and Engineering and is a member of the Boards of the Australian Partnership for Advanced Computation and of the Smart Internet CRC.

Gary E. Strong is director of the Queens Borough Public Library in New York City. In September 2003, he will assume the post of university librarian at UCLA. Before his appointment at Queens in 1994, he served 14 years as state librarian of California, where he created the California Research Bureau, the California Literacy Campaign, and the Partnerships for Change program. Most recently he was named 21st Century Librarian by the School of Information students at Syracuse University, received the Charles Robinson Award from the Public Library Association, and was named Business Person of the Year by the Queens County Chamber of Commerce.

Jens Thorhauge is director general of the Danish National Library Authority, a government agency responsible for administration of Danish library legislation, library development, and some central national library services such as www.library.dk and Denmark's Electronic Research Library. Before taking his current position in 1997, he was director general of the Danish Library Association. He also served for many years as a teacher, researcher, and consult at the Royal School of Library and Information Science.

Preface

What will the library of tomorrow be, and what should it be? Such questions may not be new in the history of libraries, but at the turn of the twenty-first century they are being raised with urgency and purpose. A rapidly changing information service environment, combined with a seriously challenging financial environment, are pushing information providers—in particular, libraries—to think in new ways about how they provide information services to their users.

In organizing this conference, CLIR and the California Digital Library started from the premise that the current environment offers libraries the opportunity to re-think what they do, how they do it, and why. We invited speakers who have thought about these questions in their positions at research centers, public libraries, funding organizations, and in technology departments. Two of the speakers provide perspectives from abroad. All have much to offer as we consider new models for providing access.

This conference, the second in a series supported by Documentation Abstracts, Inc. (DAI), offers a unique opportunity for a cross-fertilization of ideas on the topic of emerging visions for access in the twenty-first century. We are grateful to DAI for making this conference possible. I am also grateful to the University of California for cohosting the event.

Deanna B. Marcum
President
Council on Library and Information Resources

Welcoming Remarks

Lawrence H. Pitts

Those of you who work with faculty know they possess a healthy amount of enlightened self-interest in addition to their dedication to society's interests. Faculty want it all, and they want it now—whether it's a book, journal, or art collection—and they'd like not to walk too far to find it. Some seem to like going to libraries simply to stroke books, and when we talk about changes on the horizon, some get a teary-eyed look. The changing economics of libraries are unfamiliar to many faculty members. The faculty do not fully appreciate the new realities, but they can be taught. They see library lists every year with journals crossed off, and even though they sometimes bargain them back on, they can see the trends.

It amazes me that when we as faculty publish something, we sign away our rights to publishers and then buy our research back at a fairly hefty price. Many faculty members do not realize that after a period of time one can put the research back into the public domain. This is a feature they never think about—they are too busy doing their next paper. The faculty truly are interested in the widest possible dissemination of their intellectual product. They are excited about what they are doing and want people to know about it. Yet today the distribution of many journals is declining because they're getting more expensive. So the distribution of much faculty work is becoming more limited. And that is also something many faculty members do not fully appreciate.

People don't like change. Faculty are familiar and comfortable with current publishing arrangements. But the realities are inescapable. California's state budget is a disaster. In the face of a $35-billion deficit, which is more than the budgets of most countries, budget cuts are a reality, and so is the rising cost of print material. Fortunately, new technology has arrived in the last decade. We have the opportunity to reduce the pain we would experience if we continue to do things as we have in the past.

Organizations such as the Council on Library and Information Resources will help us master what we need to do to move forward in this terrible crunch between rising costs and falling budgets. There are clearly issues to sort out: how to protect scientific organizations, professional societies, and the university presses. We still need publishers, and they somehow must make enough money to stay in business, so finding the right business models will be a challenge.

There may be resistance to change from publishers. But the University of California faculty make up about 10 percent of Elsevier's editorial boards, and if they turned to electronic publishing, it would send a powerful message. The universities and university librarians also might resist change. Libraries are ranked in part, for example, according to the number of volumes owned. How do you deal with a system in which not all of the nine (soon to be ten) campuses can have collections the size of Berkeley or UCLA? If the faculty at all campuses can get all the books they want, very quickly, what does it matter if the book resides at their campus or not? We are embarking on a series of exploratory meetings with the faculty and librarians to discuss how to move forward. Oddly, the bad budget situation may be auspicious, because without it, things would move a lot slower. We may ultimately benefit from these lean times.

I am sure that changes will take place in other segments of the library sciences and information resources world as well. Public libraries, for example, must be under intense budgetary pressures. It is an interesting time. Technology gives us wonderful opportunities—I greatly look forward to seeing how we change in the years to come.

Reaching across Library Boundaries

*Robert S. Martin**

When Dan Greenstein and Deanna Marcum asked me to participate in this important event, they told me that the goal of the conference is to stimulate new thinking among the conference participants about the possibilities for library services. And they suggested that the program and discussion here would focus on visions that emphasize deep resource sharing, collaboration, and effective and innovative uses of technology. I accepted the invitation with alacrity because these are issues that are of great interest to me personally and to the Institute of Museum and Library Services (IMLS), which I represent. I am not certain what I can contribute to stimulating new thinking in these areas, but I do have one or two thoughts that I am happy to share with you this evening.

What are the new possibilities for library services that we need to be thinking about? It seems to me that the possibilities are enormous, limited only by our ability to imagine new permutations and combinations and to articulate the benefits that we can hope to produce for the society that we seek to serve. But I would like to focus my remarks on two broad themes that I think can provide the foundation for fostering imaginative innovation and for articulating our value: the opportunities and challenges in building digital libraries and the social role of libraries. In the process, I hope to discuss some obstacles that lie in the way of achieving new visions of library services.

Digital Libraries Bring Collections to Life

The first theme that I would like to address is the development of digital libraries. As Deanna Marcum pointed out in her address to

---

* The opinions expressed in this article are those of the author and do not reflect the policies or positions of the Institute of Museum and Library Services or the federal government.

the Elsevier Digital Libraries Symposium in Philadelphia in January, the time has come for us to "build massive, comprehensive digital collections that scholars, students, and other researchers can use even more easily than they use the book-based collections we have built up over the centuries."

She went on to identify the three general characteristics of the digital library of the future. She said it will be

- a comprehensive collection of resources important for scholarship, teaching, and learning;
- readily accessible to all types of users, novices as well as the experienced; and
- managed and maintained by professionals who see their role as stewards of the intellectual and cultural heritages of the world (Marcum 2003).

So where are we now in terms of achieving this vision? In the past decade we have made substantial progress in creating large-scale digital collections. It is extremely important, however, to distinguish digital collections from digital libraries. As Cliff Lynch pointed out at the IMLS WebWise conference at Johns Hopkins in 2002, a clear consensus still does not exist about what exactly constitutes a digital library. Digital collections are "raw content," Lynch said, while "digital libraries [are] the systems that make digital collections come alive, make them usefully accessible, that make them useful for accomplishing work, and that connect them with communities." The collections alone are nothing but a bunch of "stuff." They have value only when surrounded by a matrix of content and interpretation that makes them useful. This is a significant issue: we need to be certain that we are developing digital libraries, not just digital collections.

When we do that, when we take care to surround collections with appropriate metadata supplying context and interpretation, then we truly develop synergy. The whole becomes greater than the sum of its parts. Lynch resurrected a remark attributed to Marvin Minsky many years ago, proposing a scenario in which someone in the future will say: "Can you imagine that there was a time when the books in a library didn't talk to each other?" (Lynch 2002). Now we have an environment in which the books in a library can in a real sense talk to each other. And that has the effect of making the whole greater than the mere sum of individual books put together.

How do books talk to each other? The simplest example is the one we have all encountered on Amazon.com, when you order a book and the site tells you, "If you are interested in that book, then you might also be interested in these titles." Our bibliographic systems make those connections implicitly now, but you have to know how to ask for them. We have the capability to create these links proactively now.

When books talk to each other, though, they can also talk to outside systems and programs and even people. And if individual books can talk to each other, then certainly libraries can talk to each other. I am not sure we can yet quite fathom all the implications of that phenomenon.

Digital Technology Changes Our Thinking on Copyright

One of the greatest impediments to realizing the potential of universal access to digital collections, it seems to me, is our current system of protecting intellectual property rights. The system works reasonably well—albeit not perfectly—in the traditional analog environment. Transferring the concepts of copyright to the digital arena, however, raises numerous thorny problems.

This complication really should not be a surprise. Our current system of copyright is, after all, a relatively new innovation in human history, arising from a very specific set of circumstances. In the manuscript era in the West, there was no notion of intellectual property rights. Texts were freely copied as the primary form of distribution, or "publishing." Far from objecting to such copying, authors—if they were aware of it at all—welcomed it as an indication of the influence of their ideas or appreciation for their creativity.

Indeed, what we know as copyright arose only after the advent of typographic printing made it possible to produce manifold copies of a text quickly and cheaply, and when the market for many copies created an economic stake for the author (as well as the printer or publisher). The purpose of copyright, after all, as enshrined in the U.S. Constitution, is "to promote the Progress of Science and useful Arts." This purpose is achieved "by securing for limited Times to Authors and Inventors the exclusive Right to their respective Writings and Discoveries" (art. 1, sec. 8). In other words, to encourage authors and inventors to continue to be creative and inventive, authors and inventors get to keep (for a limited time) whatever earnings accrue from their work. Upon this rather simple foundation an extremely complex system of law has evolved. But the purpose of that law remains "to promote the Progress of Science and useful Arts": that is, to promote a social good.

Digital technology, though, raises complex and perturbing questions about these rights and about the very nature of copying and reproducing copyrighted material. In the digital arena, it is all too easy to make and distribute widely unauthorized copies of protected material. The content industry and rights holders, as a result, have tried many different approaches to plug the hole that digital technology has created in our structure of protections. The current statutory structure has been stretched, twisted, and distorted in an effort to extend it to cover products of a form never originally intended.

After all, in the words of the statute, "Copyright protection subsists . . . in original works of authorship fixed in any tangible medium of expression" (*Copyright Act*). This language is not ambiguous. It means that expression must be "fixed," in the sense that text is fixed when it is printed; the creation cannot be left in a mutable form. And it also means that the creation must be embedded in a physical object; it cannot exist in an ethereal stream of bits. Extending the concept to cover evanescent digital media would appear to require extraordinary leaps of logic and law.

One proposed way to recognize copyright in digital media that has been widely advocated by some players in the content industries would be to mark all commercial digital content in some way—with a string of bits or with watermark technology. Developing mechanisms to find and read the marks, however, would require a broad range of technological innovations. Such marking technologies would need to be standardized and might require government regulation. Large segments of the information technology, consumer electronics, and communications industries would have to radically restructure their products to incorporate the technology.

Another proposal is to make many classes of hardware and software untamperable—that is, difficult to modify, or "closed." But most recent technical innovation has been fostered by open platforms such as the PC and the Internet. The Internet as we now know it, the World Wide Web, Linux and other open-source software, and graphical browsers all have resulted from innovation made possible by open systems.

Indeed, such limitations would alter the very nature of the Internet as we know it. The Internet was developed to provide a mechanism for computers to share data on a distributed, decentralized network. Peer-to-peer file trading did not begin with Napster—it is a fundamental part of the Internet's design. Digital music files are just another kind of data.

Moreover, copying data is inherent in computer operations of all kinds. Computers copy data constantly, from one part of RAM to another, from RAM to magnetic storage and back again, from RAM or storage to video displays, and so on. And digital copying is the very foundation of the Internet, in which data are typically divided into "packets," which are then copied and recopied from computer to computer until reproductions of all the packets reach the destination computer and are reunited into a perfect copy of the transmitted information.

As the Napster episode indicates clearly, society has not yet established a norm regarding copying and sharing materials on the Web. History provides many examples of the failure of law to prohibit behaviors about which there is no established social consensus. (Prohibition is perhaps the most obvious example.) It is not clear that any of the newly developed legal edifices attempting to extend our copyright structure into the digital arena—such as the Digital Millennium Copyright Act (DMCA) and the Uniform Computer Information Transactions Act (UCITA)—will indeed prove workable. And yet, copyright has many useful elements. It is difficult to argue that it should be jettisoned. But until a workable approach to addressing intellectual property rights is developed, we cannot realize the potential of digital libraries.

Rethinking Preservation in New Library Strategies

One of the biggest impediments to the long-term development of a comprehensive digital library is the issue of preservation of digital materials. Actually, this is a case where I think the term *preservation* itself obscures the issue. We in the library world are quite familiar with the overall issue of preservation of library collections in the traditional sense. Usually this approach focuses on the difficult but concrete concerns over preserving physical objects, such as paper documents, or reformatting them in a proven preservation medium like silver halide microfilm so that the information they contain can be maintained indefinitely. There is no way to use this approach in the digital arena. Instead, we might use alternative language, such as *persistence* or *sustainability*.

I think the best way to frame the concept, however, is to talk about transmission over time. Networked digital information technology is very good at transmitting data across space, but it is not well suited for transmitting data across time. The evanescence of the medium creates many difficulties.

First of all, there is the problem of the lack of fixity in digital media. One of the greatest advances occasioned by the advent of typography was that, for the first time, readers of a given document could be assured that they were all reading the same document (more or less). Prior to the advent of typography, readers of a manuscript document could have no confidence in the reliability of the text they were reading. It had probably been transcribed by hand many times and was many generations removed from the original text. Many kinds of errors and variations, both intentional and unintentional, may have been present. Moreover, because of the variations in formats of each exemplar of a text, there was no reliable means of citation. The advent of fixity facilitated a major advance in scholarly communication, the importance of which is difficult to exaggerate.

In a digital medium, that fixity is lost. One can have no assurance that a digital text conveys the original expression of an author. It may have been altered, intentionally or unintentionally. And with many document presentation schemes, we have even lost the reliability of citation formulas.

Beyond this problem with fixity lies the problem of fragility of the media. Random access memory (RAM) is completely evanescent and transitory. Most digital files are stored on magnetic media. These media are inherently unstable and must be refreshed on a regular schedule. The longevity of other media for digital storage (such as laser-encoded discs like CDs) remains uncertain, although we can be pretty confident that they are less stable than paper codices stored in an appropriate environment.

Another concern is that in order to record, store, and retrieve digital files of any kind, we must become dependent on specific hardware and software. The operating systems, application programs, and digital data encoding schemes have already gone through many generations of evolution in the short period since the advent of digital information technology. Most of these result in mutually unintelligible file structures. The simplest example is the rapid change in simple word processing application programs. WordStar was once the dominant commercial program for text processing. Nowadays, if you have a disk with a WordStar file on it, even if the disk itself has not deteriorated, and even if you have hardware that will read the disk, it is now impossible to retrieve a WordStar text file without a sophisticated translation program. Indeed, it is even difficult to retrieve and edit a file that was written in an earlier version of Microsoft Word. Imagine how this problem cascades over time with the constant development of new application software.

In spite of a lot of work addressing these issues at the National Archives and Records Administration (NARA) and the Library of Congress (LC) over the past two decades, little real progress has been made. A new white paper by Brian Lavoie at the Online Computer Library Center (OCLC) provides an interesting approach to the economic issues related to digital preservation and may pave the way for finally developing a decentralized approach to addressing this problem.

Funding the Digital Library Takes Diverse Resources

As Deanna Marcum has pointed out, creating digital libraries is very expensive. The library community's initial response to suggestions that we might create a comprehensive digital repository was that, inter alia, this development would be impossible because it is too expensive. Where will the money come from?

There are now a number of different federal sources of funding for creating digital content. IMLS, as the only federal agency specifically authorized by statute to support digitization of cultural content, has provided significant funding for digital projects in recent years. The National Science Foundation, through its Digital Library Program, has provided substantially more funding. The National Endowment for the Humanities has recently begun providing support for digital projects under its Preservation and Access program. The LC has done much, not only in digitizing its own collections but also in supporting digitization effort more generally.

A number of foundations and corporations have also provided resources to support the effort of developing digital materials and understanding their use. The Andrew W. Mellon Foundation in particular has been very active in this area.

Heretofore, the costs of creating and managing digital collections, coupled with the enormous scope of the project, have inhibited the development of large-scale digital collections. Now, however, we are beginning to see that as the technology continues to develop, costs of digitizing and storage are coming down. The goal may indeed be within our grasp.

The most interesting recent development is the growing recognition among elected officials that the benefits of creating comprehensive digital collections may be worth the cost. One approach that starts with an interesting premise is the Digital Opportunity Investment Trust (DOIT). Originally suggested by Lawrence Grossman and Newton Minow, founders of the Digital Promise Project, DOIT would set aside anticipated revenues from resale of the broadcast spectrum as an endowment for creating digital resources to support education. The idea is sort of a twenty-first century Morrell Act, which supported the development of the land-grant colleges in the nineteenth century.

According to the official literature distributed by Digital Promise, "DOIT's charge will be to unlock the potential of the Internet and other new information technologies for education in the broadest sense; to stimulate public and private sector research into the development and use of new learning techniques; and to encourage public and private sector partnerships and alliances in education, science, the humanities, the arts, civic affairs and government."

Foremost in the list of activities to be undertaken by DOIT is "Digitiz[ing] America's collected memory stored in our nation's universities, libraries, and museums to make these materials available for use at home, school, and work." Thanks to Congressman Ralph Regula (R-OH), who led the effort, the fiscal year 2003 appropriations bill directs $750,000 to the Digital Opportunity Investment Trust. These funds will be allocated through the Federation of American Scientists and are to be used to create a proposed structure for DOIT and to develop a research and development roadmap to outline the steps necessary to fulfill the Digital Promise.

There are alternatives to massive, centralized federal funding that are worthy of consideration. Many of us, especially those in academic libraries, are already aware of a phenomenon that I call "the *other* digital divide": for many of our users, especially students, but increasingly faculty, if it is not digital, then it may as well not exist. Students waiting until the last minute to write a term paper (emphatically *not* a new behavior) will simply not use library resources that are not already digital. And faculty teaching in the online environment will likewise rarely incorporate into their lesson plans anything that cannot be loaded up on, or linked to, their WebCT or Blackboard courses. We have already come to terms with the fact that Web-based instruction, originally developed for distance-learning initiatives, is now commonly used to support teaching and learning in traditional course environments, a phenomenon that only strengthens this trend.

This phenomenon has the potential to lead us in a different direction as we seek funding models for developing digital collections. A decentralized, demand-driven model might be the best approach. Traditionally we have provided users of our unique archival collections photocopies of such materials to support their research needs and have had no reluctance to charging cost-recovery fees for the privilege. We are now altering that strategy, using scanning technology that simultaneously provides a hard copy for the patron and a digital file for the library. If carefully structured and managed, an approach of scanning-on-demand, with cost recovery built in, can result in the development of significant digital resources at low public cost.

Institutional repositories are another very important and promising element in creating a comprehensive digital library. The California Digital Library provides one excellent example of this approach. The synthesis of Cliff Lynch's recent observations on digital repositories in the Association of Research Libraries' (ARL) February 2003 *ARL Report* provides the best summary to date of the issues surrounding institutional repositories. I commend it to your attention and incorporate it by reference rather than dwell further on that important topic. I might add that institutional repositories are not restricted to academic and research libraries. They are also relevant to public libraries, which can serve as gateways to local governmental information and community resources. They can also serve as repositories for the work of independent scholars, free-agent teachers, and independent self-directed learners.

New Evaluative Systems Show the Digital Library's Value

In all sectors of public life we are experiencing an increasing emphasis on assessment and accountability. This is in my view quite understandable, and it is appropriate. And it is not really new. As John Cotton Dana said in 1920:

> All public institutions . . . should give returns for their cost; and those returns should be in good degree positive, definite, visible, measurable. The goodness of a [library] is not in direct ratio to the cost of its building and the upkeep thereof, or to the rarity, auction value, or money cost of its collections. A [library] is good only insofar as it is of use . . . . Common sense demands that a publicly supported institution do something for its supporters and that some part at least of what it does be capable of clear description and downright valuation. (Dana 1999)

IMLS has provided training to all grantees in outcome-based evaluation and requires grantees to develop outcome-based measures for the success of their projects. We simply have to do a better job of demonstrating the value that we provide to the communities we serve. This doesn't mean that we have to quantify everything—good stories are important, too.

Evaluating digital resources is difficult. One of the traditional criteria for evaluating libraries, especially in the research university environment, is size of collection. This is, after all, a common-sense approach to determining how well a library can meet the needs of a large and complex body of users—by anticipating their needs.

ARL has been collecting and using a wide range of statistics to measure library services. In the past, those measures relied heavily on counting inputs. The comprehensive ARL index is derived from a multiple regression algorithm that converges on size of collections and expenditures.

In recent years, however, recognizing that the utility of this approach has limitations, ARL began its New Measures Initiative. The initiative was undertaken in response to the increasing demand for libraries to demonstrate outcomes and impacts in areas important to the institution, coupled with the increasing pressure to maximize use of resources.

This initiative includes an approach toward defining and measuring library service quality across institutions and creating useful quality assessment tools for libraries. It also explicitly attempts to provide realistic ways to measure the quality of access versus ownership and to explore the feasibility of defining and collecting data on the use and value of digital resources. Efforts such as these are essential if we are to fully realize the potential of digital libraries and adequately articulate the value that they bring to the communities we serve.

Responsibility for Learning Rests with the Community

I would like now to turn to my second theme, which is the fundamental social role of libraries in the twenty-first century. At IMLS, our focus is on the educational mission of museums and libraries. This focus drove the creation of the institute in its present form six years ago—the simple recognition on the part of some members of Congress that museums and libraries share a fundamental educational mission: supporting learning. The mission of IMLS is to build the institutional capacity of museums and libraries to provide resources and services that support learners of all ages. In short, we are dedicated to creating and sustaining a nation of learners.

Libraries of all types provide a broad range of resources and services for the communities they serve. They preserve our rich and diverse culture and history and transmit it from one generation to the next. They provide social settings for numerous community activities. They support economic development. They provide extraordinary opportunities for recreation and enjoyment. And they serve as a primary social agency for education, providing resources and services that both support and complement agencies of formal education.

We often hear it said that libraries (and librarians) select, organize, retrieve, and transmit information or knowledge. That is true. But those are the activities, not the mission, of the library. Certainly we perform those activities, but the important question is: To what purpose? We do not do those things by and for themselves. We do them in order to address an important and continuing need of the society we seek to serve. In short, we do them to support learning.

Perhaps it would be better to say that libraries—all libraries—are in the business of creating and sustaining learners of all ages. We live in an information society, but today, in the twenty-first century, we must do more than merely live among information. We must create a learning society.

We enter this twenty-first century in the midst of a bewildering mix of opportunity, uncertainty, challenge, and change, all moving at unprecedented speed. Fueled by dazzling new technologies, increasing social diversity and divide, and radical shifts in industry and labor markets, accelerating change has become a way of life. As Daniel Pink has recently observed, we live in "a world of accelerated cycle times, shrinking company half-lives, and the rapid obsolescence of knowledge and skills. In a free agent economy, our education system must allow people to learn throughout their lives" (Pink 2001).

Pink goes on to cite the development of the World Wide Web as a prime example of the power of individual learning and the limitations of formal education:

For example, how did anybody learn the Web? In 1993, it barely existed. By 1995, it was the foundation of dozens of new industries and an explosion of wealth. There weren't any college classes in Web programming, HTML coding, or Web page design in those early years. Yet somehow hundreds of thousands of people managed to learn. How? They taught themselves—working with colleagues, trying new things, and making mistakes. That was the secret to the Web's success. The Web flourished almost entirely through the ethic and practice of self-teaching. This is not a radical concept. Until the first part of this century, most Americans learned on their own—by reading. Literacy and access to books were an individual's ticket to knowledge. Even today, according to my own online survey of 1,143 independent workers, "reading" was the most prevalent way free agents said they stay up-to-date in their field. (Pink 2001)

In recent years we have seen a marked decrease in traditional schooling, the rise of home schooling, and an increase in individualized, self-directed, free-choice learners. There is a growing trend toward decentralizing education, a trend that has been termed by some "schooling" education. These trends present an enormous opportunity for libraries and museums, which have always excelled at providing resources and services that nurture and support informal learning. In this environment, the development of comprehensive digital collections, in both museums and libraries, has the potential to revolutionize the way we think about teaching and learning.

For the past several years, we at IMLS have been engaged in an initiative that we refer to under the heading of "The 21st Century Learner." Our purpose is to address the need for bold new models of integrated action among formal and informal educational institutions in meeting the demands and interests of learners in the twenty-first century. We are particularly interested in the potential for museums and libraries to inspire such action in their communities.

At the heart of this discussion is a central thesis: The responsibility for learning is not the exclusive preserve of formal educational institutions—schools, colleges, and universities. It is instead a community-wide responsibility. Learning throughout the lifetime should be a continuum, with formal and nonformal learning opportunities complementing one another. Learning does not start at the schoolroom door; neither does it stop at that portal either. It is ubiquitous.

As this 21st Century Learner initiative has developed within the IMLS, based on a central vision, it has been built on a ladder of premises that directly affect our work with museums and libraries. These six premises are as follows:

- In a knowledge-based economy, learning across the life span is becoming increasingly essential.
- As lifelong learning becomes more central to our society, museums and libraries have new opportunities to serve as vital learning resources. Their unique assets already establish them as trusted community resources.

- The central challenge is awareness: to establish greater public awareness of and access to these resources, and awareness of how to use these resources most effectively to foster critical thinking and enhance information literacy skills.
- To meet this challenge, museums and libraries may be most effective by becoming part of an infrastructure or network of learning resources—schools and universities, public radio and television, community-based educational activities—all sharing a common educational mission.
- Technology today provides us with new tools for supporting such collaborations
- Finally, well-defined learning collaborations, designed to meet the changing needs of the twenty-first century learner, ultimately will enrich and strengthen the quality and fabric of community life.

Collaboration Is Essential to Twenty-first Century Success

At IMLS we believe that collaboration is emerging as *the* strategy of the twenty-first century. Collaboration aligns with how we think about our communities as "holistic" environments, as social ecosystems in which we are part of an integrated whole. The kind of collaboration I have in mind in the strategy for the twenty-first century is not a joined-at-the-hip symbiosis. It is instead a mature and reflective recognition of intersecting nodes of interest, activity, and mission. It is the potential for creating synergy out of cooperation, building a structure in which the whole is greater than the sum of the parts.

Librarians have a consistent history of collaboration. Sharing resources is fundamental to the practice of the profession. Indeed, the concept of sharing underlies the very foundation of the modern library as a social agency. Libraries were established in order to pool scarce resources for the common good. The society libraries of the Colonial period arose from the simple fact that books were too scarce—and too expensive—for any one individual to be able to acquire access to all he or she needed, so readers brought their individual collections together to share them in common. This ethic of sharing has remained strong in the practice of American librarianship ever since.

Collaboration, however, is not easy. It requires that we—as individuals and as institutions—behave in ways that are not "normal," that feel unnatural. My favorite definition of collaboration is that it is "an unnatural act, practiced by nonconsenting adults." My dictionary, in fact, offers the following as one definition: "cooperating treasonably, as with an enemy occupying one's country." This notion may be at the heart of some of the difficulties that we encounter in attempting to collaborate. A better definition for our purposes is "working together in a joint effort."

Differences among institutions, however, can be profound. The assets and personnel, academic preparation of professionals, even the very vocabulary we use to describe operations can all be dramatically different. The characteristics and proximity to the communities served can vary widely. Values and assumptions of mission and service can also be different.

In short, the cultures of organizations can differ dramatically. These differences are real, they are challenging, and they do not go away. It is imperative that these differences be recognized forthrightly. Over time, they can evolve into sources of synergy rather than contention.

At IMLS we are, naturally, interested in fostering collaboration between and among museums and libraries. It is inherent in our structure and mandated by our governing statute. But we also think it is imperative to reach out beyond the museum and library to find nodes of intersecting interest and mission among other players in the community.

One of the potential partners in which we have the most interest at present is public broadcasting. Robert Coonrod, the president of the Corporation for Public Broadcasting (CPB), gave the keynote address at our recent WebWise conference in Washington. He provided a broad overview of the changes that broadcasters are going through, due in large part to the impact of digital technology. Those changes lead to the inescapable recognition of a pending convergence. Public broadcasters are becoming more and more like libraries and museums—just as libraries and museums are becoming more and more like broadcasters.

Coonrod encouraged us to begin to explore what he called "community-based public service media collaboratives." We already have ready examples of such collaborative projects in the landscape, many of them funded by IMLS. We are now actively exploring collaborative projects at the meta level between IMLS and CPB.

To give you an idea of how essential we think this kind of approach is to success, you should know that we have recently created a new position on our staff, director for strategic partnerships. The charge to that officer is to identify opportunities for useful collaborations with other federal agencies, with nongovernmental organizations, with other funders such as foundations and corporations, and with the relevant service organizations. We have agreed to define the long-term success of this approach when these agencies start to come to us for help in involving museums and libraries in their programs because they recognize what museums and libraries can do to help them achieve their goals. That has already begun to happen.

Community in the Brick-and-Mortar Library

Lest all this discussion of digital libraries leave you with the impression that I think libraries will cease to have a physical presence in the future, I want to address the important role of libraries as a place in the community.

The biggest challenge to libraries in the twenty-first century, it seems to me, is to balance traditional roles and services with the new roles and services afforded by digital information technology. It is absolutely essential to recognize that the new technology has not replaced the old. It has instead opened a new range of opportunities for service, created new populations of users, and made possible new modalities for carrying out the unchanged mission of libraries to support learners of all kinds. The critical point to remember is that while libraries are increasingly digital, they also remain essential physical places in the community.

An excellent example of the challenge of this duality came to the fore in an incident in Tacoma, Washington, last fall. In response to a critical budget shortfall, the Tacoma City Council was preparing to cut the library budget and close several library branches. Councilman Kevin Phelps asserted that "we have to embrace significant change in how we look at libraries.... The current libraries, as we see them today, are somewhat of a dinosaur." To Phelps, the growth of the Internet and the home computer meant that libraries did not need to be physical places. "The current model we have is very intensive on bricks and mortar," Phelps said, commenting on the 10 neighborhood branch libraries in the system. Instead, he wanted to foster a single central library, with services distributed to the public digitally. Phelps's colleagues on the council were reported to have congratulated him for "thinking outside the box" (Callaghan 2002).

Peter Callaghan, a Tacoma *News Tribune* columnist, was not persuaded. "Let's think inside the box for a moment," Callaghan wrote. "Because it is inside those brick-and-mortar boxes where community lives. Tacoma's 10 libraries are the living rooms of 10 neighborhoods. They are places where latchkey kids can feel safe in the afternoons, where community groups have meetings, where seniors go to read papers and stay current, where people without Internet access at home go online, where parents give their children the gift of reading" (Callaghan 2002).

Mr. Callaghan has it exactly right, it seems to me. We must embrace and pursue the potential of universal access through comprehensive digital collections. But we must not lose sight of the indispensable role of the library as a place, a place that builds social capital and supports a civil society; a place that is a vital and vibrant center of community life—whether your community is an isolated rural village, an impoverished city center, an affluent suburb, or a research university.

Libraries in the twenty-first century have a unique and critically important role to play in providing resources and services that create and sustain a nation of learners. If we work to build comprehensive digital collections that are appropriately organized and presented for ease of access, if we focus our efforts on developing resources that support learning of all kinds, and if we demonstrate the value that we create and provide for the communities we serve, then we will succeed in fulfilling that promise.

References

Callaghan, Peter. 2002. Councilman's plan to cut city libraries is far from courageous. *The News Tribune*, Tacoma, Wash., October 1. Available at http://www.tribnet.com/news/local/story/1872253p-1986445c.html.

Copyright Act. U.S. Code. Vol 17, sec. 101.

Dana, John Cotton. 1999. *The New Museum: Selected Writings by John Cotton Dana*, edited by William A. Penniston, Introduction by Stephen A. Weil. Newark, N.J.: The Newark Museum Assn.; Washington, D.C.: American Association of Museums.

Lavoie, Brian. 2003. *Incentives to Preserve Digital Materials: Roles, Scenarios, and Economic Decision-Making*. White Paper. Dublin, Ohio: OCLC Online Computer Library, Inc. Available at http://www.oclc.org/research/projects/digpres/incentives-dp.pdf.

Lynch, Clifford A. 2003. Institutional Repositories: Essential Infrastructure for Scholarship in the Digital Age. *ARL Report*. Issue 226 (February).

Lynch, Clifford. 2002. "Digital Collections, Digital Libraries and Digitization of Cultural Heritage Information." Web-Wise 2002: A Conference on Libraries and Museums in the Digital World, March 20-22, 2002. Available at http://www.imls.gov/pubs/webwise2002/wbws02.htm.

Marcum, Deanna. 2003. Requirements for the Future Digital Library. An address to the Elsevier Digital Libraries Symposium, Philadelphia, Pa., January 25, 2003. Available at http://www.clir.org/pubs/archives/dbm_elsevier2003.html.

Pink, Daniel H. 2001. School's Out: Get Ready for the New Age of Individualized Education. *Reason* (October). Available at http://reason.com/0110/fe.dp.schools.shtml.

THE LIBRARY AND SOCIETY

The Personal Library: Integrating the Library in the Networking Society

Jens Thorhauge

The topic of this symposium, visions for access in the twenty-first century library, embraces a broad range of problems that are primarily technological and organizational. Some of these problems can be discussed in terms of new roles for the library in civic society. I will focus on presenting an organizational model for developing library services based on a strategy for seeing all libraries as cooperating partners in a coherent system rather than as single institutions.

A Shortage of Means for True Access

The basic vision for access that I probably share with most of my colleagues is not new. It can be expressed most concisely as access for everybody to all published material, no matter how it is stored. At least for print, this vision has been behind the International Federation of Library Associations and Institutions' (IFLA) core program, Universal Availability of Publications (UAP), for decades. The vision further proposes that the material be presented and organized in a way that makes it easily accessible for as many groups as possible. Access should be integrated into daily life, with the ultimate goal being what I perceive as "the personal library," which generates information resources from a specific individual profile that is then linked with a library service. A third element in the vision deals with learning facilities, such as easy access to library-organized computer and information literacy programs. The fact that these basic visions are not very new underlines the fact that they are not yet realized, and how to achieve them remains an open question. Hence I welcome this symposium and the opportunity to present what I call "the Danish Model," a framework in which libraries change their organizational nature to come into line with the information society. Technologies can then become networking partners in a coherent system, even in traditional fields such as collection building. My basic point of view is this: We do not lack visions for access in the twenty-first century. What we do lack are efficient means to realize them.

This concept of one coherent library system is simple to understand, but not easy to achieve. The concept was developed in a small country where we are forced to merge resources to find the most efficient solutions, but I see no reason not to think along the same lines in large countries as well. The one-system concept is based on the conviction that today's and tomorrow's demands for easy access to information can be met only by very large libraries or groups of libraries, and the more they cooperate to create these services, the more user-friendly they will be. Letting all libraries work together, then, is necessary to enable effective access to information, but it is also a question of cost-effectiveness. In a small country such as Denmark, "all libraries" should be taken literally. In large countries, a federal approach in some areas seems to be relevant, while in others a state or regional approach might be more appropriate. Regardless, this one-system vision is a major challenge to traditional institutional thinking and cultural behavior. Obviously it is not possible to establish such a new organizational platform overnight; it needs time and strategic planning.

New Roles from Traditional Skills

Before I move further into presenting the Danish model, let me offer a few general remarks about emerging roles for the library, also illustrated by the Danish example. The first clause in the *Act Regarding Library Services*,[1] passed by the Danish Parliament in 2000, states:

> The objective of the public libraries is to promote information, education, and cultural activity by making available books, periodicals, talking books and other suitable material, such as recorded music and electronic information resources, including Internet and multimedia (Part I, sec. 1).

The mission of promoting information, education, and cultural activity has been integrated in the first paragraph of the Danish library laws for nearly half a century, and it can be found in library statements and legislation from many countries. My point is that the basic mission for libraries has not changed for a very long time. Libraries give access to information, the raw material for knowledge that the World Bank considers to be the most important factor in creating and maintaining welfare states. Libraries are cornerstones in building democratic, enlightened populations; they are linked to research and education at all levels; and they promote culture and support the building and maintaining of cultural identities. Basically, the mission of libraries in the civic society is to help people manage and improve their lives, the key words here being *learning, understanding,*

---

[1] English translation of the act can be found at http://www.bs.dk/publikationer 2.ihtml?id=1346.

insight, and *inspiration*. This is traditional knowledge, but it has to be reinterpreted too often to be understood properly.

The really new element in the quoted clause above is, of course, new media and technology. It indicates that a library is no longer defined as a collection of books but as an institution giving access to information, regardless of the format or medium in which that information is stored. This shift in the definition implies a major change in how the library's mission is fulfilled. The new methods can also be expressed in terms of defining new roles for the library. The Public Libraries Mobilising Advanced Networks (PULMAN), a European Commission-funded project, is made up of leading public libraries from nearly all European countries. In a manifesto issued in March 2003, PULMAN defined the following four supporting roles for public libraries:

- democracy and citizenship
- lifelong learning
- economic and social development
- cultural diversity[2]

How these roles are defined and discussed has evolved in the last 10 years, but the idea that libraries support democracy and active citizenship by supporting the education of people on all levels dates back to the period of Enlightenment in the second half of the eighteenth century in Europe and the United States. And while the impact of information and knowledge on social and economic development has likewise been broadly recognized at least since the dawn of industrialism, the idea of lifelong learning is probably the newest concept for libraries' role, even if activities in libraries have in practice long supported what is today understood as *lifelong learning*. For instance, you will find in many countries a popular concept of the public library as the people's university.

Does this notion indicate that new roles are not emerging? I don't think so; rather, the idea is that we develop new roles from traditional skills. Let me give some examples of how this development can work. The most revolutionary way comes when we try to integrate access to information in everyday life through Web-based services such as Web-based catalogs, linked collections, Internet guides, subject gateways, and, of course, full-text access to as many records as possible. We produce and add value to information, making the proper information more easily accessible. We also establish and run programs on computer and information literacy, and we likewise support informal learning and self-help in all areas. Most libraries try to integrate traditional activities such as the promotion of reading and culture into their programs, and through this integration, they often find new ways to explore possibilities.

A Danish scholar defined the roles of the public library in terms of four different centers: information, learning, cultural, and social centers (Andersson and Skot-Hansen 1994). All of these roles may

---

[2] Full text of the manifesto can be found at http://www.pulmanweb.org/news/PULMANconference_manifesto.htm.

be subdivided by organizing access in the most convenient way for more specific purposes. A fine example of that organization can be seen in San Francisco, at the main public library, where you will find centers on jobs and careers, business and technology, Afro-American culture, and gay and lesbian studies.

The Danish Model[3]: Libraries and Government Agencies Cooperate under the Law

The Danish model's philosophy and library concept do not vary fundamentally from those in other democratic welfare states with developed library systems. The difference lies in the organization and its effect in producing results more quickly and more extensively than in many other countries working with the same objective in mind. The basis for the model is updated legislation in the form of a framework law, combined with the presence of a government agency that regulates activities that encourage development and cooperation. The number of programs offered has led to a paradigm shift, as the library offers ever more specific virtual services.

Denmark is an old, wealthy but small country with only 5.2 million inhabitants. Because Denmark has been a kingdom for more than 1,000 years, surrounded by the sea on all sides except for some 40 miles bordering on the north of Germany, the culture is extremely homogeneous. The language spoken is Danish, a language in which some 16,000 records are registered every year in our national bibliography. Sixty-four percent of the population are public library users, half of them on a monthly basis. Eighty-one percent of all children are public library users, and all schoolchildren are users of school libraries. Eighty percent of the population have Internet access. More than 100 research libraries network on virtual services primarily for campuses, as displayed in Denmark's Electronic Research Library.

The primary responsibility for public libraries is placed at the municipal level, while government research libraries as a rule are integrated in the university or other institution that they serve. Only the county library function, which is government funded, is subject to regulations by way of performance contracts between the Danish National Library Authority and the municipalities that run the county libraries, which support public libraries throughout the county by means of interlending, advice, and continuing education. All primary schools have school libraries, which are obliged by law to cooperate with the local public library.

Danish libraries are moving toward the vision of one coherent library system, but progress is incremental, and the conflict between the traditional library concept and its working culture and the networked library of the information society is openly acknowledged.

I will briefly present some of the elements in the Danish model,

---

[3] Further elaborated in Thorhauge 2002a. A shorter introduction to the Danish library system can be found in Thorhauge 2002b. Ongoing development can be followed in the journal *Scandinavian Public Library Quarterly*, edited by the Danish National Library Authority. The electronic version is available at www.splq.info.

with the *Act Regarding Library Services* being the most important one. Since 1920, Danish public library activities have been regulated by national legislation, up to this latest act, passed in 2000. The act is based on the hybrid library concept and is meant to create the framework for meeting users' needs in a networked information society. It explicitly states that libraries will work together on interlibrary loan (ILL), as state and county libraries must share their collections through ILL free of charge, even for the requesting institutions. Likewise, public libraries and school libraries are obliged to cooperate. All core services are free of charge, which means that all kinds of access to library materials are free for everybody, and all libraries should maintain their collections. All municipalities, even small ones with less than 5,000 inhabitants, run a professional library service.

The act also states that all libraries should give Internet access and e-access to their services, while the state should require Web-based access to the union catalog. This access could be seen as another cornerstone in the Danish model. For the last 10 years, the union catalogs for public, university, and other research libraries have been merged into one database, the DanBib-base, containing bibliographic records on all holdings in Danish libraries, amounting to 17 million records. This database is the platform for the new national Web portal to Danish libraries, bibliotek.dk (www.library.dk).[4] Through this portal, you can search and request any title in Danish libraries bought for lending. You can choose any library to pick it up from, and if the book is in print, you may even buy it through this Web site. In some areas, you may also order a delivery service for a fee. In the field of lending cooperation, the library.dk service realizes the vision of a coherent library system. Under this Web service lies a well-functioning distribution system that efficiently delivers the titles requested to the library selected; the database is organized so that requests are routed to the nearest library. And for the user, library.dk is a coherent system, requiring only that one pick up a virtual basket and choose books, articles, CDs and videos, then request or order them.

The portal also contains a growing number of full-text records, and the vision is that more and more bibliographic records will give immediate access to full-text versions with a single click. The portal is more than a search-and-request database; it also gives access to some 20 Web-based services. A good example of networking among different libraries can be seen in the way the e-reference is organized. Forty libraries participate, and while most participants are public libraries, a growing number of university libraries have also joined. Questions can be asked by chat, mail, or phone 84 hours a week. While the number of users and the number of participating libraries is increasing, the number of local reference desks is decreasing. An e-reference service for children is also a success. Other services include subject portals and gateways that lead to a variety of resources, from

---

[4] Further information in English is available from www.library.dk and in Andresen 2001, Andresen 2002, and Hansen 2003 at bibliotek.dk.

links to licensed material, such as encyclopedias and other kinds of digitized content. Music, art, food, medicine, and transportation are all subject examples. You will also find a virtual children's library, called DotBot, on the site. A number of special information services are provided here, including resources for immigrants and ethnic minorities; a fiction e-zine; and an e-encyclopedia on living Danish fiction writers, produced by a network of libraries that contains portraits, updated bibliographies, and text examples.

A third element in the model is the role of the government agency—the Danish National Library Authority (DNLA) (not to be confused with the national library)—which is significant in developing libraries, public as well as academic. The agency is the government's central advisory body in the field. It handles a number of administrative tasks; responsibilities include running the public-lending right scheme (which distributes $20 million to Danish authors each year, thus being an important factor in securing a literary production in Danish); compiling library statistics; and maintaining standards, including classification and cataloging rules.

Developing People and Systems Together

The most important of the agency's emerging roles is its responsibility for developing the library system. This duty is fulfilled in several ways, all the while building on a vision to enhance the hybrid library and more effectively integrate services into the everyday life of a growing number of users. The agency has run strategic development programs in four fields: support to technological development, development of new services, competence development of library staff, and a change of the library system structure itself. Along with the new *Act Regarding Library Services*, the DNLA received a three-year grant to implement the new library concept. The money was spent according to the four strategic cornerstones.

Let me briefly run through the programs. The technological development program, the first cornerstone, was intended to make all libraries capable of networking with their users and with one another. Next, creating new services is crucial to changing the roles of libraries. The national portal, bibliotek.dk, described above, is the essential new service, being initiated and constantly developed by the DNLA. The portal also gives access to a number of services such as e-reference and Internet guides. These services are produced and run by networked libraries. New services in general are developed as projects, supported by the DNLA.

Building new competencies is the third strategic cornerstone. The aim of this effort is to ensure that staff members educated decades ago are qualified for delivering and developing adequate services in the networked library. The real challenge was to spend the money in such a way as to produce permanent change. As I believe that the challenge of developing competence is global, I will outline our program. We did four things: focused on new leadership, trained trainers, trained project managers, and started to build an information literacy program.

In general, Denmark offers some very good courses and seminars in the field of continuing education. The Royal School of Library and Information Science is the main provider, with some 300–400 yearly courses offered throughout the country.[5] We decided to initiate a number of activities with a different scope. First, we focused on the need for new leadership, the need to change institutions into learning organizations, introducing networking and team building, developing new professional roles for the staff, and changing attitudes to traditional priorities in the library. A one-and-a-half year diploma-level course was organized, and nearly half of all Danish public library directors participated. We will continue this effort, but future courses will cater to directors of both research and public libraries.

The second idea, training the trainers, was based on the desire to give each person working in libraries an opportunity for annual training. Since county libraries are responsible for identifying and meeting needs for competence development in their service area, they were asked to organize training for experienced staff to help colleagues setting up new services, such as Internet classes or a music department, or to help them contribute to networked, Web-based services. Trainers should run simple courses on the spot and work for a couple of days with colleagues in their library. Since the program began, some 100 trainers have been trained.

A third idea was training project managers. This program was based on the experience that project work seemed to be one of the best means to develop competencies and that nearly all new services start out as projects. Eighty project managers are now available as a result of our training.

The discussion on information literacy and library programs emerged with these initiatives, and a first step was taken to offer courses aimed at giving all libraries a professional background to provide civic society with an information literacy program.

The fourth strategic effort relates to a change in the structure of the library system that is crucial to achieving the goal, as presented in my initial remarks, of creating one coherent library system. Four major activities have been going on here. We supported municipalities financially if they agreed to merge their library systems with those of other municipalities, creating larger units that could cope with networking on national services better than small libraries. These municipalities could then develop staff and establish new services in the hybrid library.

We also changed the county library structure, keeping the existing 16 libraries but changing their tasks and roles to match the demands of Web-based services. New tasks were related to develop new competencies in the libraries in the county and play an advisory role in creating new services.

---

[5] For more information on the interaction between the Danish library development project and the continuing education program at The Royal School of Library and Information Science, see Larsen 2001.

We supported financially the building of new networks, producing new services in cooperation not only with libraries but also with other kinds of institutions. And last, but not least, we managed to create a networking cooperation between university and other research libraries to deliver virtual services. This cooperation is expanding into areas besides the virtual, and the first steps to cooperation on the virtual library between research and public libraries have been taken.

A last, very important element for DNLA is the running of Denmark's Electronic Research Library, which is a full, working virtual library built on the cooperation of more than 100 research libraries and coordinated by DNLA. The virtual library gives password-based access to 9,000 e-journals, subject gateways and link collections, and library catalogs (a virtual catalog working closely with library.dk). Retroconversion of catalog cards is nearly completed, and digitization programs are currently running.[6] As my subject here relates to the civic society, I will not venture further into this area except to mention it as part of the Danish model and state that a huge challenge exists in fostering closer cooperation between research and public libraries.

Creating New Libraries and New Librarians

I hope that the model I have outlined suggests some solutions to the challenges of organizing more integrated access to information resources. Focusing mainly on the organizational aspect, I have not discussed at all, for instance, the problems libraries have with copyright, which is an important issue in relation to future access. Let me just mention that we focus on the same problems with aggressively rising prices of e-journals as do libraries in the United States. We have worked with alternative open-source models such as the Public Library of Science, but we have also had very positive experiences with license-based access.

I would like to conclude by pointing out what I see as three major challenges to libraries in the coming years.

The first is the challenge for the library to be the e-information provider. To provide total access to electronic information, on various conditions, is the ultimate goal. Because this aim is very difficult to achieve at the moment, what we can do—just to mention a few activities—is to work with ongoing digitization programs to provide more flexible licensed, password-based access to e-content and to establish systematic access to material of a public nature, for such material where rights holders are positive toward open-source approaches. In Denmark we offer this increased accessibility by providing more and more full-text material through the bibliotek.dk catalog. Library-organized Web distribution of films and music is another new challenge still on an experimental level but that will be a

---

[6] More information on Denmark's Electronic Research Library can be found on its site, www.deff.dk, and on the information site, www.deflink.dk.

task for the coming decade. Offering e-reference and hotline services on a 24/7 basis is only a question of obtaining the resources.

The second major challenge is to create the library as a place that really embraces local needs. As virtual services have changed the behavior of library users, we have to develop the library as a place to meet the needs of our users in a way that differs from the book-oriented library of the twentieth century. We must provide excellent space for information centers and for various types of learning activities as well as for cultural center activities. We shall go on developing programs to meet needs of lifelong learners, but we should also be aware of the need for informal meeting spots and inspiring nonprogram areas.

The third major challenge is to create the new librarian. The most important step here is to transform the librarian from an information provider into a knowledge provider; that is, from someone who merely gives access to information to someone who more actively supports the user in acquiring the needed knowledge. This change will be manifest in a variety of new roles for librarians: information producers, portal editors, community information specialists, information literacy trainers, trainers in the learning library, coordinators and advisors for children's culture, consumers' rights advocates, and still as subject specialists in all fields.

All these challenges could be summed up in the ultimate vision of creating the personal library, updated according to a chosen profile and giving immediate access to the references. We will achieve such a level of access, but only step by step and by networking on new organizational premises.

References

Andersson, Marianne, and Dorte Skot-Hansen. 1994. *Det lokale bibliotek: afvikling eller udvikling*. København: Danmarks Biblioteksskole.

Andresen, Leif. 2001. A New Route to Danish Libraries. *Cultivate Interactive* 5 (1 October). Also available at http://www.cultivate-int.org/issue5/danish/.

———. 2002. Visit Your Library from Home. *Scandinavian Public Library Quarterly* 1: 4-5.

Hansen, Lone. 2003. Immediate Access to Danish Libraries. *IFLA Newsletter to the Sections on Interlending and Document Supply* 31 (1): 31-34.

Larsen, Gitte. 2001. Developing Skills for New Electronic Services in Libraries. *Scandinavian Public Library Journal* 34 (4).

Thorhauge, Jens. 2002a. *Danish Library Policy: A Selection of Recent Articles and Papers*. Copenhagen: Danish National Library Authority. Available at http://www.bs.dk/index.ihtml?side=http://www.bs.dk/publikationer2.ihtml?id=2302.

Thorhauge, Jens, ed. 2002b. *Nordic Public Libraries: The Nordic Cultural Sphere and its Public Libraries*. Copenhagen: Danish National Library Authority. Available at http://www.bs.dk/publikationer2.ihtml?id=2248.

Libraries Empower People to Participate in a Civil Society

Gary E. Strong

On reflection, I should have perhaps titled my remarks this morning, "*Librarians* Empower People to Participate in a Civil Society." It is the commitment and dedication of our staff at Queens Borough Public Library that have built our programs and engaged our very diverse population. We as librarians are often called upon to think about the future. But in the past few months, thinking about the future has become more difficult. As we concentrate on the drama played out before us each evening, the future seems uncertain. As we face shrinking resources for support of libraries, museums, schools, and communities, our resolve is stretched to the limits.

Urban public libraries in America today are helping shape the future of our cities. They provide the capital by which people can empower themselves, governments can govern, and communities can be peaceable. As the Library's social role in this new century takes form, we are challenged to create and sustain services that bridge the past and the future.

A Fundamental Public Good

New York City is a unique urban center. It comprises five boroughs and is served by three separate public library systems. The Borough of Queens is considered the most racially and ethnically diverse county in the United States. Total population recorded in the 2000 U.S. Census topped 2.2 million people, a 14.2 percent increase over the past decade. Forty-six percent of the total population are foreign-born and speak a language other than English at home. Among the children in our public school districts, about 140 different languages are spoken in addition to English. Approximately 27 percent (some half-million people) of the population five years and older consider that they speak English less than "very well." Such is the diversity of ethnic and immigrant communities living and working in Queens that a seven-mile subway line connecting Times Square and Flushing has been nicknamed "the International Express." Each stop on this elevated line introduces passengers to a variety of ethnic communities within different neighborhoods, reflecting the multitude of nations from around the world.

Queens Library ended its fiscal year on June 30, 2002, having circulated 16.8 million items and welcomed more than 16.3 million visitors to its Central Library, 62 branches and 6 adult learning centers. Our collections have grown to more than 9.8 million items. More than 24,000 programs were attended by 529,000 library customers in that year, and staff answered 4.5 million reference and informational questions.

The library of the future is not a simple place; it is a multifaceted, multicultural organism. In Queens, this belief is supported by our mission: "to provide quality services, resources, and lifelong learning opportunities through books and a variety of other formats to meet the informational, educational, cultural and recreational needs and interests of the borough's diverse and changing populations." The mission further states that the library "is a forum for all points of view."

Further, we believe in our vision. The Queens Library represents a fundamental public good in our democracy. It assures the right, the privilege, and the ability of individuals to choose and pursue any direction of thought, study, or action they wish. The Library provides the capital necessary for us to understand the past and plan for the future. It is also our collective memory, as history and human experience are best preserved in writing. The Library is dedicated to the needs of its diverse communities, its advocacy and support of appropriate technology, the excellence of its collections, the commitment of its staff to its customers, and the very highest ideals of library service.

We at the Queens Library believe deeply in equity and that libraries are fundamental in empowering people to take charge of their lives, their governments, and their communities. In this way, Queens Library has an essential role to play in the new millennium. The collections we build, the access we provide, and the technologies we embrace will carry the people of Queens into a productive and creative future.

Marketplace Techniques Meet Traditional Services

Our leadership team focuses on four strategic directions for the Queens Library: (1) state of the art libraries, (2) books and reading, (3) quality customer service, and (4) children and teens. Strategies within each area have been identified for further development by various work teams. This work drives our budget and resource allocation, particularly in these difficult budget times. We will continue to build both the collections and the connections that we have put in place.

Our challenge has been to merge the successful aspects of our traditional popular library services with those of the emerging electronic information marketplace. We will continue to provide a "sense of place" in each of our communities. People come to our libraries as a social and personal experience. We are seeing teens coming in record numbers, primarily for the technology. But they also come to find books to read, attend poetry slams or open-mike nights, participate in book discussion groups, and attend other programs. We will continue to celebrate the book and promote reading. We will support creativity and intellectual inquiry. We will continue to be a learning organization.

At the same time, we will use technology to connect to the world. As we develop our online presence, we will be aware that we are not an "e-business." Libraries have always been about the selection of the best in books and quality in our collections from all over the world. Moving into the electronic arena, we must find ways to guide our customers to useful information and helpful sites in the electronic village. As we search to provide a safe environment for kids and their families, we work to support an individual's freedom to pursue any direction of thought and study. We will develop methodologies to select quality Internet sites in the major languages spoken in the community and create navigation aids that move customers to information that serves their needs. Through video teleconferencing, we connect children in after-school programs to the world.

Speaking the Neighborhood's Languages

In the traditional library, we build quality collections and place appropriate collections in the various neighborhoods of the borough. Each neighborhood has a different mix of nationalities and languages. Rather than make each branch a small version of the Central Library, Queens asks managers to assess their communities and build collections to meet their needs. Multilingual collections are not limited to special centers, but can be found in every branch that serves an international community. We maintain 152 collections in 24 languages across the system to meet the needs of our customers. Popular books, periodicals, newspapers, music CDs, videocassettes, and DVDs keep people connected with their homelands and languages. These collections are "merchandised" in bookstore fashion and encourage browsing. In addition, we offer extensive collections of materials to help immigrants learn English.

Special resource collections are built and maintained in the Central Library (70-plus languages) and at the International Resource Center (IRC) (44 languages) that supplement local branch holdings with more serious material. At the IRC, collections are limited to works about countries and cultures represented by the language of the collection. In the French collection, for example, all of the nonfiction is about France or francophone countries. And fiction and literature include only works written originally in French.

Programs of ethnic and performing arts are presented in communities across the system, including free readings, concerts, and workshops. Free lectures and workshops in the most widely spoken immigrant languages of Queens are presented on topics essential to new immigrants' acculturation, such as citizenship and job training information, advice on helping children learn, and information on social services. Our *Directory of Immigrant Serving Agencies* assists the library staff and other organizations and governments in identifying useful and helpful services for those newly arrived in the city.

Our programs attract very diverse audiences. Typically two-thirds of the audience will reflect the target community; the rest come to learn about their new neighbors. We see new immigrants regularly in our traditional programs to learn about living in America and their new community. The family is very important in Queens, and we focus many of our efforts on providing an experience for the whole family. For example, in celebrating the Lunar New Year, we will have programming for the whole family, and families often come and spend the whole day with us. Recently children in one of our branches engaged in a Web chat with children in Zagreb, Croatia, part of an ongoing dialogue with one of our sister libraries.

The IRC also presents programs in the performing arts. In fact, we have presented some of the finest Chinese opera companies, direct from Shanghai and Taipei, as well as Taiwan's Tsou Aboriginal Dance Troupe. But our emphasis, which is unique in Queens Library, is lectures and seminars that address social, political, medical, philosophical, and religious issues. Geographically, East Asia has been a constant focus of these programs. Last October, a panel of distinguished speakers from Beijing, Shanghai, Taiwan, and the United States—including Wang Dan, a former student leader of the Tiananmen demonstrations—spoke about the future of China. And last month, Cao Siyuan, a Beijing-based economist who led a successful campaign to institute a bankruptcy law in China, gave his views on China's future.

With Korea in the news, former U.S. Ambassador to South Korea Donald Gregg spoke on U.S. foreign policy toward the two Koreas. Next month, James Seymour of Columbia University's East Asian Institute will speak on the North Korean refugee community in China.

The Library also sponsors a Chinese book discussion group that meets regularly in both the Flushing branch and the IRC. Branch and IRC staff members select the Chinese-language books for the groups, and discussion is conducted in Chinese.

The Library's adult learning centers provide opportunities to learn English as a second language, to improve English language skills, and (for native-born Americans) to gain basic skills. Small conversation groups and computer-assisted instruction greatly expand these opportunities for learning. Classes are often oversubscribed, and there are long waiting lists for services.

Our galleries are often host to prestigious exhibitions from other libraries and countries, including the National Library of China, Shanghai Library, Korea, Iran, and Russia. The current exhibitions focus on fine art from Russia, and a wonderful photographic exhibit sponsored with the Chinese American Museum of New York City spotlights scenes from the Flushing community.

Access to all Queens Library collections is through the Library's OPAC, InfoLinQ™. Terminals are available to customers in all public service areas of the library. Readers of Spanish, Chinese, Korean, and Russian have the option of clicking on bibliographic instruction pages displaying Roman and vernacular character sets. All public access terminals have Internet access, and terminals are used system-wide by customers to access Chinese-Japanese-Korean (CJK) publications, online news services, and other databases. Customers can manage their own accounts, place holds, or ask reference questions using the Library's Web site.

The Queens Library introduced WorldLinQ™ in 1996. WorldLinQ™ is a multilingual Web-based information system providing location of information through appropriate Web links around the world of interest to our customers. There are currently modules in Chinese (including Taiwan, Hong Kong, and Mainland China), Korean, French, Spanish, Russian, Romanian, and Ukrainian. Sites in Arabic, Croatian, and Urdu are in development.

Our International Relations Office coordinates relations with libraries around the globe. The office negotiates and manages cooperative agreements with libraries and library organizations nationally and internationally. Currently we have partnership agreements with libraries in Asia, Europe, and Latin America, including the National Library of China and the Shanghai Library. Staff members from these libraries have worked in Queens as part of an exchange program, and members of our staff have worked in their libraries. Members of our staff have participated in a variety of visitors programs sponsored by the U.S. State Department, most recently visiting American Corners libraries in Russia.

Our International Center for Public Librarianship advocates the North American model of public libraries and creates on-the-job-training opportunities for library professionals. Under this program, a number of librarians and graduate library students from around the world have worked as interns and fellows in the Queens Library, 30 in this year alone. They spend between one and six months experiencing tailored curricula to meet their individual interests and needs. These activities engage our staff to learn about libraries in other countries and to gain an understanding of the newly arrived customers that we serve.

Building Partnerships within the Community

As a major community resource, we build partnerships with others serving our borough's populations, most significantly the Queens Health Network. We are both concerned about the condition of health services in Queens. Together we make a significant impact on getting information on immunization, asthma, and cancer. We have just finished a basic literacy class for workers at the hospitals who needed to improve their English language skills. We are also working closely with the Department of Labor and manage the resource center at the Jamaica One-Stop, helping people find new employment. With the Justice Department, we are piloting new library services for at-risk youth in two communities.

Public libraries are not dead and are not dying. We see more people today than ever before. They come to enjoy our collections, to meet in our spaces, to experience public dialogue, to read books, and to use the new technologies that we are making available. We often see people within days of their arrival in America. I often ask, "How did you hear about the Queens Library?" and hear the answer, "Someone told me to come to the Queens Library when you arrive, and they will help you there."

One thing is certain: We may not be facing an easy future, but we will be engaged in one that is exciting and challenging. Most important, we will need librarians who can rise to the challenge of merging the traditional print-based library services with those of a virtual nature. We will need librarians who understand human behavior and value public service.

We are particularly challenged today by our diverse communities. Libraries can play an instrumental role in the development of a civil society by providing broad-based access to traditional and electronic resources. Creating a level playing field for all in our communities will ensure that our democracy thrives.

Toward Supported "Communities of Interest" in Digital Environments

Robin Stanton

The future of the library is a topic of great importance for the higher-education sector as well as for the library sector. I bring a university perspective to the topic. My focus is on developments in higher education and the influence of these developments on university libraries. I assume that university libraries will adapt to change in education and research institutions as they are transformed through the digital revolution. Many libraries, whether in higher-education or not, are strengthening their education missions in their own right. However my focus today is on universities, on the need for change in their information services, and on the broader range of services which university libraries might provide in meeting that need.

The Library Enterprise Faces the Future

Emerging visions—the library of the future, or the future of the library—is a topic without boundaries. Two key questions have focused my thinking. First, what futures are enabled for the library by the remarkable development of digitized text, visual, and audio materials and by the equally remarkable development of global, undifferentiated, end-to-end digital communications? Second, what are, for want of a better term, the "business models" for one future rather than another? By business models, I mean to include desirable objectives, strategies, and—most important—feasible funding arrangements.

The library enterprise, construed broadly as services that preserve and make available published and valued information, is coextensive with what we have come to call the global civic information infrastructure. But this infrastructure and the library are quite different enterprises. My comments will focus on a third enterprise, the academic enterprise, a venture largely prescribed by education, research, and research training. I keep these three enterprises—the academic, the library, and the information infrastructure—distinct in my mind, even though they are often conflated when the impact of technology on higher education is discussed. It is easy to see why they are often intermixed, especially when the focus is on libraries and universities, given that universities institutionalize pursuit of the academic enterprise. But in so doing, universities also become major contributors both to the library and to information infrastructure enterprises. It is in our interest to understand these entanglements, to separate concerns, and to be as deliberative as we can about the information services that support the academic enterprise, whether they be sourced in library agendas or elsewhere.

University Objectives for Digital Assets

Because institutions can be conservative to a fault—in the university sector at least—we have yet to rebuild resource-allocation processes and to take into account the value of the new generation of support services for the academic enterprise, otherwise so tantalizingly close at hand. Many of our problems arise from not having reviewed and restructured the way in which we manage our resources. Not surprisingly, consideration of business cases for servicing the academic enterprise quickly leads to consideration of the role of institutions and how they behave. Institutions can play a vital role in creating libraries of the future, and it is a role that they are destined to play.

Sometime soon, many universities will adopt the following objectives in one form or the other:

- They will manage, preserve, and provide open access to their digital assets. Managing digital assets internally includes managing rights for others to use these assets. We are already involved in managing information on the corporate side of universities through content management systems, including metadata issues that are similar to, and in fact overlap, metadata challenges associated with scholarly information.
- Universities will preserve digital assets that are judged to have long-term value; how they make those judgments will become clearer with time.
- Universities will provide open access to their digital assets, including elevation of these assets into global access platforms; develop digital asset holdings in line with their strategic interests; and foster and sponsor national and global communities that will be built around education, research, and research training.

None of these objectives is new, but each of them needs to be qualified by the extent to which they will—or will not—strengthen individual institutions. I believe that adopting these objectives will strengthen most institutions, and that such action, in turn, will create the need for services that are quintessentially associated with librarianship. National interests sometimes surface in this agenda; however, the drivers are international in character.

What issues are raised for our institutions in pursuing these objectives? It is clear that new services are involved and that those services will require skills that are not readily found in our current service base, including libraries. I expect librarian-based services will emerge that embody those skills. Further, while library facilities will continue to have a strong physical presence for campus-based education programs, the services we are thinking about must be available when and where they are needed, and many of them will be projected through the information infrastructure.

Moving toward Communities of Interest

Because significant shifts in funding for services are unlikely, introducing new services will mean displacing existing ones. This displacement is likely to be difficult if we do not build programs for staff development—for academics and students as well as technical support staff—to take us there. We have to get our heads out a few years, see where we are going, and make sure we can go there with our values intact. We also must make sure that these values come from the broad community.

To meet these objectives, academics will need to become engaged in information management processes. Discipline-specific judgments are required. The paramount need, as I see it, is to build academic practices while introducing new services. This combined approach argues for "communities of interest," a notion to which I assign an explicit place in the strategies for moving ahead. In the sense I use it here, "communities of interest" are broadly defined as the academic communities that have common or cognate research methods inasmuch as those methods depend on particular information services. The distinctive needs of musicologists and visual anthropologists in working with sound and imagery, respectively, are examples of such communities.

Digital technologies are the drivers for change in library services. They are disruptive; otherwise, we probably would not be here talking about these issues, and they are arguably the most enabling of all the technologies shaping our social and economic systems. Change over the past decade is astounding, and the pace of change continues to increase. Possibilities for the future appear boundless. Not so long ago, the call for digitization programs was a familiar one. The vision was simple: Encode our information sources and digital databases, either by conversion or digital creation, and much of the promise of the information revolution will follow or, at the least, become possible.

We are still at an early stage of converting existing information sources to digitized forms. The world, however, now has a burgeoning layer of digital data, much of it contained in the global information infrastructure. In part because of the vast quantities and ongoing proliferation of data generated, we are developing a sharp focus on the need to understand how data can be structured, valued, integrated, preserved, and accessed through purpose-driven discovery processes. The purposes here are the higher-education purposes.

Validation, Creation, Discovery, and Preservation: Prescriptions for the Institutional Community

These challenging dimensions of data management become considerably more complicated when the rights of creators and owners are taken into account. Higher-education institutions have a special interest in ensuring these challenges are met, especially for information whose authority stems from scholarship. Scholarly information is validated within academic communities. That point is made frequently and in a number of ways, but this concept needs to be kept in mind: By and large, we do validate our own information sources.

Creativity is deeply respected in academic communities, and the traditional open publication of scholarly works has provided ready access to ideas for the wider community. Boyer's classification of scholarly activities—that is, his four scholarships of discovery, teaching, integration, and application—helps us appreciate the broad range of materials involved in scholarly activities and to which we assign high value in-house. This range has expanded dramatically. Traditional papers and manuscripts are now accompanied by data sets, programs, compositions in audio and visual domains, and a wide range of multimedia objects. The extent of this expansion and the variety of forms scholarly works take are straining the traditional peer-review processes on which validation of materials rests.

Indeed, the meaning of the term "scholarly publication" has been set adrift. Universities build, nurture, and foster scholarly communities. They secure and manage financial resources and provide physical and informational infrastructure in support of those communities. The wherewithal to create, collect, store, discover, organize, preserve, and access scholarly materials is a vital part of a university's support. Is there a boundary between the academic and the library enterprises? I do not know the answer to that question. In the past, there has not been too much of a division, and I hope that there will not be a boundary in the future.

Creation of scholarly materials excepted (admittedly a big exception), responsibility for information management has largely been institutionalized through facilities and services set up in commons, with libraries having the frontline responsibility. Within this model, all the aspects of information management other than creating—in other words, collecting, storing, discovering, organizing, preserving, and giving access—are going to be changed dramatically by digitization. That change is happening already. Our institutional structures, however, will also change in the divide between the commons and the rest of the university, and that divide is very important.

The evolution of skills and expertise underpinning traditional library services has been strongly conditioned by print technologies and the relatively shallow, largely discipline-independent information structures upon which organization and discovery of information have been based. This is, of course, the case more for published materials than it is for primary material collections, the latter usually involving a deeper understanding of content. Primary materials or not, support for organization and discovery of print objects at the infrastructure level has been built around catalog structures and strongly encapsulated print objects.

The Consequences of Digitization for the Academy

I want to consider three consequences of the emerging digital framework for the academy. First, digital objects may not be strongly encapsulated. They are inherently compound objects, having internal structures that can readily be exported to the discovery-organizational-access processes. Given sophisticated indexing mechanisms, which we do not yet have, parts of a digital object can be reused. Boundaries among objects in broad collections are blurred by a sharing of subcomponents. These boundaries can almost disappear or be multiply determined according to specific purposes to the queries, ownership, or rights restrictions.

A second consequence is that academic processes are increasingly being conducted in ways that depend on digital-to-digital processes. This dependence, in turn, leads to incremental publishing and to the need to consider the information structures within and between digital objects early in research and education programs, rather than in the dissemination phase.

Third, publication of the wide range of digital objects associated with education and scholarly research leads to the need to attach comprehensive descriptions of great integrity to individual objects and especially to objects that are not otherwise self-defining. I am thinking here well beyond the normal metadata discussions and considering the emerging ontological dimensions.

With these three consequences of digitization in mind, it is not difficult to envisage the new services that we need to introduce to serve academics better in this digital world. Will librarianship embrace the information professional skills that are being pointed to here? I hope so. I expect so. In any case, broadening the skills base to include the design and specification of the information structures is an obvious need, as are the skills to define access and rights-management structures.

It is less obvious how to address the need to have information professionals contribute to the design in the early stages of research and education programs. The viability of university-wide services is weakened as direct involvement in individual programs is increased. On the other hand, it is not practical to fund all these programs as a single entity, including having information professionals as team members of all projects as a matter of course. This has led me to focus on building communities of interest. This approach is not revolutionary, but it does invite a focus that I think we should strengthen. More important, communities of interest provide an approach to resolving the tension between individual programs and university-wide services.

Australian National University: One Institutional Approach

It is difficult to prescribe the impact of information technologies on universities. However, we can aim to create responsive institutions and learn from one another as to how we might do so. For this section of my talk I have drawn on the pathway the Australian National University (ANU) has chosen. University organization structures per se are not particularly relevant to the cause; accordingly, my comments will refer to functional aspects of the ANU's experiences.

The ANU promotes a three-component functional model which includes platforms, communities, and services, and that focuses on bilateral relationships among the three components. Platforms are the enterprise-level systems—repositories and operating processes, and their links to the national and global information infrastructure—used to support academic communities. The service component comprises skills and expertise that, on the one hand, assist communities in using the platforms and, on the other, assist in developing the platforms to better support research methods and outcomes associated with particular communities. The expertise and skills needed in the services component guide us to the expanded roles of information professionals needed for the university library of the future.

The ANU's first move in responding to the impact of information technologies occurred in 1999–2000, when it carried out a major review of information policies—a process that most universities have performed over the past decade. Our institutional goals for the academic enterprise were used to drive objectives for our information infrastructure; again, a quite common approach. We then looked at support services, not only scholarly services but also corporate services. All universities involve people working in multiple roles—research, teaching, learning, and administration. We tracked the major roles in which any individual was involved and then mapped out the dependency between scholarly and corporate information services. The trends showed us that teaching and learning—even research, to some extent—are increasingly dependent on corporate as well as scholarly information. Accordingly, we set about coordinating these previously separate areas to provide a broad set of academic services supporting both classes of information.

We also recognized the need to build staff training and information literacy programs. We have since put such programs in place; however, they are resource-intensive and will require restructuring within service budgets if they are to be sustained. The main outcome, at least from the perspectives of governance, organization, and coordination, was to create an information portfolio to sit alongside the portfolios for research and education. Under this arrangement, university strategy and policy formation involve information agendas as one of three major portfolios.

To complement portfolio arrangements, the university created an Information Strategy Committee as a subcommittee of the Academic Board. Then to run strongly coordinated programs across campus, a converged, single budget, Division of Information was established.

The division is responsible for converged services covering four areas: scholarly information (including libraries); corporate information (including enterprise systems); scholarly technologies; and information technology infrastructure. Coordination aside, the main purpose of putting these areas together under the Division of Information and giving them a one-line budget was to balance resource allocation and priority setting.

A Planning and Strategy Framework for the Information Infrastructure

For planning purposes, the academic enterprise meets the information infrastructure under, for want of better names, e-research and e-education headings. This division reflects major funding lines and strategies for many universities. Figure 1 illustrates this structure.

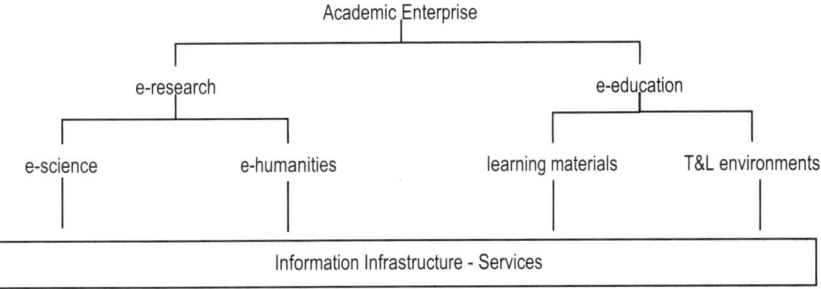

Fig. 1. Planning and Strategy Framework for the Information Infrastructure

The level below research and education reflects divides that, although contingent in nature, are driving infrastructure development in many universities. At the ANU, services in support of these two broadly defined communities currently involve different skills and have different priorities for developing platforms. In any case, communities of interest within these two major headings are emerging, and are engaging the information infrastructure more deeply in carrying out their research.

In broad terms, the science community is at a more advanced level of digitization, and is more comfortable with its scholarly communications being mediated by networked repositories, than is the humanities community. The difference can be quite stark, with science academics expressing delight with change in areas where humanities academics express deep concern. In part, this difference has developed because the sciences have been able to invest more resources in digitization than have their colleagues in the humanities. However, differences run deeper than this. The importance of computational laboratories, sharing of research data sets, and time to publication have moved infrastructure toward the sciences. We have developed high-performance computational laboratories and large-scale storage facilities linked by broadband networks. Data grids are springing up across the world and access-grid nodes are now fairly common at research-intensive universities. A thorough exposition of the role of infrastructure for major scientific ventures in the future is provided in Atkinson et al. 2003.

On the humanities side, the same future is in prospect, but it just lags a bit behind. *New-Model Scholarship: How Will It Survive?*, a recent report by Abby Smith of the Council on Library and Information Resources, provides an overview of the emerging strength of the humanities in the digitized world.

Learning materials are a major focus on the education side. From an institutional services point of view, it is a difficult area because of the cost of producing quality materials. Although the publishing industry is energetically exploring business strategies, materials currently being injected into learning environments include a wide range of institutionally produced documents and related digital objects. In addition, students locate and retrieve materials from the global information infrastructure using generalized discovery mechanisms rather than local library catalogs, even though the latter are online. This experience is widespread in education institutions. Learning environments, most based on Blackboard or WebCT, have become enterprise systems in their own right and are typically integrated with companion staff and student enterprise systems.

When one looks across the service needs to support each of the intersections in the foregoing diagram, the wide range of skills and expertise required in the service component is apparent. It presents a challenge for information professionals in universities, be they librarians, educational technologists, multimedia producers, or systems analysts.

Priorities for an Evolving Infrastructure

I often talk with my colleagues about evolving our infrastructure and about the best information environment they can imagine. In the e-sciences, for example, the major services people want are high-performance computing, collaborative visualization, cooperative environments, information access, and online instruments. At least three of these service categories—collaborative visualization, cooperative environments, and information access—are now being integrated into traditional library-based services. In the process, information professionals who can work across the broader spectrum are emerging.

On the e-humanities side, content creation and resource discovery matter most. The emergence of content management systems is viewed enthusiastically, and free-ranging discussions about the strength of text encoding and XML are commonplace. Other priority areas for institutional support are resource description schema, metadata encoding, learning management, library systems integration, and digital preservation. These topics are targets for services that we need to put in place. Preservation is, of course, a difficult problem. If we look out far enough, we hope that it will not be as hard to in fact achieve a reasonable degree of preservation as it appears to be from the perspective of the wide range of currently unsolved problems. The issue is clearly underrepresented in the multitude of "one-off"-funded digitization projects across the world. Under the resource discovery heading, questions are commonly raised about persistent identification. There are different views on this topic, as between persistent URLs or other, more content-indexed approaches. As in many other areas, awareness of the issues is more important than specific solutions. The ability to search, both as full-object and metadata, is also important, and a difficult problem when material is locked up at the repository level or within the structure of digital objects. The goal is to build a global infrastructure that enables discovery across all interconnected repositories, subject to rights and permissions. Interoperability though the Open Archival Initiative System is a promising framework for realizing this objective.

Progress on the Pathway toward a Cohesive Information Infrastructure

At what point has ANU, as one higher-education institution, arrived? If we had not reorganized, we would not have moved nearly as far as we have along the pathway toward incorporating what we see as future library services. It is appropriate to emphasize the importance of skills development in this journey. The ANU has been quite aggressive with information literacy programs, allocating substantial resources and paying close attention to quality and participants' needs. Services will not be effective unless providers and receivers have a shared knowledge base and common expectations.

Regarding digital asset management, universities have a clear need for content management systems for both corporate and academic information. Although common platforms are not practical in many institutions, it is practical to run programs that keep metadata aligned, and there are substantial benefits in doing so. Toward open access to digital assets, repository platforms such as e-prints and Dspace are being deployed across the higher-education sector. Rights management is an open-ended problem, and systematic solutions to it are not yet in sight. Although comprehensive solutions are some way off, much can be achieved in scholarly areas through frameworks such as Creative Commons.

Preserving digital assets requires looking at those assets that are judged to have a long-term value. Judged by whom? The university and disciplinary societies can judge, advise, and influence resource allocation to preservation agendas. However, more generally, there is a great deal of archive-worthy content for which there is no effective equivalent of the heritage movements found in physical, rather than informational, domains. This preservation problem has taken its place among the major concerns associated with an information-storage fabric based on interoperating institutional repositories. Although we are fostering communities of interest and developing valued digital assets at an institutional level, we have yet to quantify the long-term costs.

Barriers to Communities of Interest

There are a number of barriers to building communities of interest with respect to information infrastructure services. A major difficulty arises because ways of valuing digital objects as scholarly "productions" have yet to emerge. Even within the academic communities that have produced them, the value of digital objects can be elusive. The question of how to value the scholarship that goes into digital object design and implementation is also fundamental.

Another challenge comes with elevating objects into international and global access platforms. We can engineer such platforms, but technologies and associated standards are at a relatively early stage. Nonetheless, the development of global access platforms is widely seen as just a matter of time, and there is a great deal of optimism that it will be "sooner rather than later," at least for public domain information

Rights management presents a problem because of the understanding that the problem will not be solved in the near future. The role that a Creative Commons approach can play has not yet been assimilated into academic culture. As mentioned earlier, preservation of digital assets is also a problem that prevents communities from emerging where they otherwise would. Finally, funding models to sustain a wider range of information professional services is critical to tailoring support for communities of interest.

National and Global Approaches

Australia is energetically developing an e-science infrastructure, informed by, and to a large extent led by, developments in Europe and North America. Through the Australian Partnership for Advanced Communication (APAC), we have a national facility for high-performance computing and associated mass-data stores (see http://www.apac.edu.au). A program for developing a national advanced research and education broadband network was recently launched. In addition, programs based on grid technologies are being planned. Globally, Australia is a partner in the Asia Pacific Advanced Network (APAN).

More generally, a national information infrastructure fund has been set up with a strong focus on scholarly communication. The National Library of Australia is playing a major role, and some of its programs are helping in the higher-education area as well. Australia also has a program, the Learning Federation, concentrating on materials for primary and secondary education.

From an institutional perspective, the value of an e-science infrastructure depends on the extent to which the academic community can use it to strengthen their research. This, in turn, depends on institutional investment in linking infrastructure and, in particular, in enabling services. Grid technologies promise to provide a systematic and integrative approach to the way information repositories, computational modeling, and communications can work together. The information world in this setting is focused on data sets and not yet inhabited by the wide range of professional information skills referred to earlier. However, the demand for such skills is substantial. E-science researchers need to be able to discover where codes are stored and to have access to ontological information.

Large data sets in the e-science world are in general not subject to systematic preservation regimes, and this in itself is a looming problem. A related problem for Australia is to understand, at a technical level, the implications of relatively remote connectivity to the rest of the world. If books are going to talk to themselves, as Marvin Minsky once explained, they had better be network-aware. This issue is another aspect of the skills base needed in campus-based support services.

The Library Enterprise Is a Rich Cultural Story

I have outlined how we need to develop services and an associated skills base for institutions such as universities to manage their own digital assets and to ensure their preservation. There is an overwhelming case for this skills base and a corresponding case for the role of information professionals in the future in higher education. The question asked by this workshop—"What is the vision for a library of the future?"—is answered in large part by this institutional need, at least insofar as the focus is on university libraries. Of course the library enterprise more generally is much broader, deeper, and richer than the university library issues which I have raised. In becoming more closely linked to research and education methods associated with campus-based communities of interest, university libraries will need to embrace a broader set of skills than they have in the past. It is open to universities and their libraries to meet this challenge.

References

Atkins, Daniel et al. 2003. *Revolutionizing Science and Engineering Through Cyberinfrastructure*. Report of the National Science Foundation Blue-Ribbon Advisory Panel on Cyberinfrastructure. Available at http://www.communitytechnology.org/nsf_ci_report/.

Smith, Abby. 2003. *New-Model Scholarship: How Will it Survive?* Washington, D.C.: Council on Library and Information Resources. Available at http://www.clir.org/pubs/abstract/pub114abst.html.

Organizations noted in text

Asia Pacific Advanced Network (APAN) http://apan.net

The Library and Education: Integrating Information Landscapes

Michael A. McRobbie

This paper sketches out some emerging visions for the twenty-first century library from the perspective of a university chief information officer. Universities play a central role in research and education, and they have a longstanding commitment to maintaining the scholarly record of civilization and to stimulating innovation. But the accelerating pace of technological change is transforming both the nature and the role of the university research library.

In the past few decades, advances in information technology (IT) have driven revolutionary changes in the ways we work, learn, and communicate. Progress in the development of microprocessors, networking, massive data storage, imaging, and software has created new infrastructures for business, academic research, health care, and social interaction and new opportunities for economic development. Internet technologies are helping us build global networks that provide wide access to distributed information. As these advances eliminate barriers of space and time, we gain increasingly more direct and immediate access to scholarly materials, to the world's rarest historical artifacts, to visual art, to recorded music, and to broadcast archives. Such monumental change demands that we reconceive our models of the contemporary research library and the partnerships necessary to help it flourish. It also requires that we rethink the roles librarians play in this changing landscape.

Let me put this challenge in its starkest form with some examples. The Indiana University (IU) Bloomington main library counts five million volumes among its holdings. If all the library's holdings were digitized, including all illustrations and graphics, this would amount to about five terabytes of information.

Until recently, this was a nearly inconceivably large amount of storage. But consider that the era of a 100-gigabyte hard drive on a laptop computer is rapidly approaching. Before long, laptops and

PCs with a disk capacity approaching a terabyte will be readily available. Within our natural lifetimes laptops and PCs will, in principle, be able to hold the entire digitized contents of large university research libraries.

The change facing our libraries is analogous to the evolution of computing. In the early days, computing occurred on mainframes tended by technological priests who served as mediators between the user and the hallowed computational space. But when distributed computing emerged in the 1970s and 1980s, the need for mediation between the user and that holiest-of-holies was eliminated. As the desktop PC provided immediate access to computational capability, the staff of the university computing center no longer focused on tending the sacred flame of the mainframe. They facilitated distributed computing. By parity of reasoning, the role of the library as a physical repository of knowledge will also be utterly transformed when virtually all knowledge can readily be accessed electronically by anyone. The role of librarians will then be to facilitate distributed access to what an individual or organization really needs to find and know in this ocean of distributed information.

But there is an even more profound transformation under way. For centuries, libraries have been seen as the bastions of civilization. In the ancient world, the library at Alexandria, a prototype for the modern research library, was the place where philosophical, spiritual, and cosmological teachings came together to create a vital cultural environment. As the first universal library, with a cataloged collection of more than 500,000 scrolls, the Alexandrian library was the ancient world's center of learning. It was where tributaries of knowledge converged, an intellectual magnet that drew the best scholars of the day. Euclid wrote geometry there. Archimedes studied math there and calculated the earth's circumference with amazing accuracy. It is where the Old Testament was translated from Hebrew to Greek.

Suppose there was in ancient Alexandria a fast, low-cost duplicating service that copied the scrolls and compressed their size. This service could make the entire contents of the Alexandria library available to anyone for the equivalent of a few weeks' salary. Imagine an ancient laptop computer with its hard drive loaded with image copies of all the Alexandrian scrolls, or a set of compact discs containing copies of the scrolls. Were that the case, we would today think of the library at Alexandria as a *museum* of scrolls. We would be thankful that the information in it had been passed down the millennia through multiple copies owned by many, many Romans.

I mention this fantastic scenario to illustrate that the digital age poses what may be the greatest challenge yet to the idea of the university research library as the citadel of civilization. In a world in which the digitized contents of whole libraries can be filed on the disk capacity of a laptop or PC, we must address critical questions about how this alters the nature and role of the modern university library and its librarians.

I would venture to say that the answer to this question is quite clear. The modern library has to become the central focus of the university's digital library efforts, and the digital library must become a central focus of the university library's priorities. We must not fund such developments on the margins of our budgets and treat them as annoying curiosities. Rather, building the digital library must be a central, core part of the library's future with base-budget funding and of equal—or perhaps even more than equal—standing with the library's more traditional mission and activities. We must encourage librarians to develop parallel skill sets that will enable them to serve users of physical as well as virtual collections. Rather than choose one world over another, librarians must have a foot in each, navigating equally well through the traditional and the digital library landscape. The name of the game is balance between the old and the new.

The twenty-first century university library can and should be a creator of new knowledge, an innovator in developing collaboratively built and collectively held digitized collections. University librarians can and must take a leadership role in today's distributed information environment, becoming increasingly more engaged in the creation, organization, dissemination, and preservation of knowledge and building affiliations with other stakeholders also involved in these activities, both within and without their institutions. The key point is this: If we are to fully exploit the promise of technology, the university itself must break down the barriers that divide its traditional decentralized units and commit to a new way of doing business. Strong partnerships between IT and the library are essential aspects of our ability to create the most productive balance between the old and the new. Digital technology can be our greatest tool in this effort. But realizing the promise digital libraries hold for our universities, and for our culture as a whole, requires us to radically rethink our model of the research library and to live and work in a new landscape of highly integrated technology and human capital.

In February 2001, the President's Information Technology Advisory Committee (PITAC) submitted a report titled *Digital Libraries: Universal Access to Human Knowledge*. The first conclusion of this report is that "the full potential of today's digital libraries to support the national challenge transformations in research, education, health care, and commerce has not been realized." While the report recognizes that "the federal government has exercised early and significant leadership in developing digital library technologies," with specific reference to the multiagency Digital Libraries Initiative, headed by the National Science Foundation (NSF), its second finding is that "the government can and should do much more to further the science, technology, and creation of digital libraries." The recommendations of the PITAC report on digital libraries are directed, appropriately, to actions that the government should take to realize the potential of digital libraries. In addition to those already mentioned, the PITAC report's recommendations include the expansion of research in new "systems for organizing online content and addressing issues related to system scalability, interoperability, archival storage and preservation, intellectual property rights, privacy and security, and human usability." The committee urges "the creation of several federally funded, large-scale digital library testbeds." It enjoins the government to "provide funding to make all public federal content persistently available in digital form on the Internet." Finally, it asks the federal government to "play a leadership role in evolving policy to fairly address intellectual property rights in the digital age."

What role can universities play in advancing these national priorities for digital library development? Universities are among the nation's leaders in IT research and development. As such they can make especially important contributions to establishing digital libraries as reliable and persistent institutions offering sustainable information resources. They are one of the nation's major innovation sectors in information technology and crucial contributors in the effort to build the IT infrastructure and services required for digital libraries to realize their promise.

What is necessary for us to accomplish that? I believe we need to address the following questions:

1. What IT infrastructure is required to underpin successful digital library development?
2. How can universities plan strategically to create digital libraries and operate them as persistent and robust infrastructure, on an institution-wide basis, in support of research and education?
3. What institutional arrangements—intrainstitutional partnerships, interinstitutional collaborations, or extrainstitutional affiliations—can most productively contribute to or benefit from successful digital library implementations?
4. In what ways will the role of the librarian and the very nature of the university library need to change?

1. Leveraging the IT Infrastructure

IU's digital library program, which has a strong arts and humanities focus, has productively built on and taken advantage of institutional IT investment normally associated with so-called big science. Here are three brief examples, based on our experiences at IU, in leveraging what is usually considered information technology infrastructure specific to scientific research to provide IT resources to scholars in all disciplines and to digital libraries.

High-performance storage systems, capable of holding hundreds of terabytes of data, were first developed for use in supercomputing centers and national laboratories, such as those operated by the U.S. Department of Energy. The primary users of these massive data storage systems have been scientists in physics and astronomy, climatology, geology, and—increasingly—in chemistry, biology, and the life sciences. At Indiana University, we have implemented a high-performance storage system with a total capacity of more than 500 terabytes with a simple, Web-based front end. This system uses a combination of disk storage and high-capacity, high-performance automated magnetic tape systems and has the capability to mirror data between our Bloomington and Indianapolis campuses over our

I-Light optical fiber infrastructure. We took deliberate steps to make this same high-performance storage system available to scholars in all disciplines and in so doing have begun providing high-performance data storage facilities to researchers for projects as diverse as conservation of endangered American Indian languages, such as the Lakota and Dakota Sioux languages; compiling digital images and other archives for a study of North American and biblical slavery; and building digital sound archives from a phonetics laboratory in the field of linguistics.

This storage facility is providing the basis for development of a digital library repository to support preservation and archiving of both born-digital and digitized content. By leveraging this resource, IU's digital library is focusing on developmental issues: metadata and file format standards, submission processes and policies, and development of the repository management layer, rather than also having to deal with providing underlying, low-level storage technology.

The availability of a massive data storage facility, coupled with the development of a digital library repository, is an important element of a project being undertaken by Indiana University and the University of Michigan to develop a digital video archive for the study of ethnomusicology. The EVIA Digital Archive will preserve video recordings in digital form at very high quality and make them easily accessible for teaching and research. EVIA stands for Ethnomusicological Video for Instruction and Analysis. This project has been funded by The Andrew W. Mellon Foundation, with the IU Digital Library Program as a key partner.

IU is the first site in the United States, and probably the first anywhere in the world, that has succeeded in building a massive data storage system that serves the entire research community, offering high-end storage services to faculty and students in all disciplines. Recently we became the largest massive data storage site of any university in the country, exceeding the data stored at Cal Tech.

My second example of leveraging investments in IT infrastructure for use by humanities scholars focuses on adapting technologies developed for scientific visualization and virtual reality to the needs of the humanities and the arts. Advanced technologies for scientific visualization and virtual reality, based on high-performance graphics computers and computer displays, have been applied to science problems ranging from the three-dimensional visualization of molecular structures to the use of virtual reality tools to display the astrophysical properties of the sun's journey through space and time. At Indiana University, the Advanced Visualization Laboratory supports both these projects, as well as many others in the physical sciences and life sciences. The university has also facilitated research in innovative interfaces to digital libraries, allowing users to navigate through a virtual space to explore collections of digital art images or other resources. IU has made a point of extending the reach of these advanced technologies and making them available to scholars in other disciplines who are not typically thought of as users of virtual reality technology. These efforts include the use of visualization and virtual reality technologies as a medium for artistic creation, thus enabling faculty and students in fine arts to combine computer technology and art in innovative ways with the goal of creating new forms of visual expression. Indiana University has installed one of the few CAVE (Computer Automatic Virtual Environment) sites in the nation. The CAVE allows researchers to explore the world of virtual reality in an eight-foot cube. The most exciting aspects of virtual reality technologies include the unique ability to generate imagery, view it in three dimensions, and manipulate it in real time. As a result, medical professionals and students use the technology to project three-dimensional radiological data as they plan intricate surgical procedures. A faculty member at IU with dual appointments in computer science and fine arts uses it to create projects such as "Syn.aesthetic," an environment where the sonic input/traces of participants create a three-dimensional score/recording of all sound created in the room. Each sound manifests itself as a virtual physical object based on the characteristics of the sound, such as volume, duration, position, direction, as though the sound had been made visible at its point of creation.

Third, IU has worked to adapt IT infrastructure to the needs of scholars using high-performance networking. Indiana University is known as a national and international leader in the field of high-performance networking. We operate the network operations center for the Internet2 Abilene Network and the Global Network Operations Center, which supports international network links to advanced research and education networks in the Asia/Pacific area, Europe, Russia, and South America. This network serves as the backbone for distributed scientific experiments that are being conducted on a scale never before possible. The Sloan Digital Sky Survey offers a case in point. The survey will map in detail one-quarter of the entire sky. It will determine the positions and absolute brightness of more than 100 million celestial objects. It will also measure the distances to more than a million galaxies and quasars. It is the most ambitious astronomical survey project ever undertaken.

In 1999 we initiated a High-Performance Network Applications Program that has provided funding for IU faculty and graduate students to develop new research and teaching applications that require high-performance local, regional, or national networks. A number of these awards went to applications in the arts and humanities. One such application is the archaeological reconstruction and rendering of ruins such as the Mayan sites in Chichen Itza and delivery of high-resolution virtual tours of these sites over computer networks. These archaeological reconstructions form the basis of the Cultural Digital Library Indexing Our Heritage (CLIOH) project, which is creating a digital archive of cultural heritage sites from around the world. Another high-performance network application in the arts and humanities is the use of networks to create shared virtual spaces for collaborative performance of musical works by musicians in diverse or remote locations. All of these applications further the development and evaluation of network-based collaborative environments for information sharing and information seeking, from virtual reality interfaces to digital libraries.

2. Planning Strategically for the Development and Operation of Digital Library Programs

Indiana University began rethinking its IT strategy in 1996, when then-IU President Myles Brand set the goal of making IU a national leader in absolute terms in the use and application of information technology. As the first step toward this goal, in 1997 IU formed University Information Technology Services (UITS)—IU's technology organization, which provides integrated information technology services and infrastructure across Indiana University's two research campuses and six regional campuses. That same year, the Digital Library Program was formed as a partnership between the university libraries, UITS, and the School of Library and Information Science. IU's new School of Informatics became a fourth partner last year.

More than 200 faculty, staff, and students worked energetically to develop our first IT strategic plan. Librarians and technology professionals had, at that point, been meeting for some time in informal discussion groups that enabled their two cultures to explore matters of mutual interest. Faculty provided substantial input from the beginning of the planning process.

Now, five years after the initiation of the strategic plan, faculty, staff, and students on all of IU's campuses enjoy IT infrastructure and services of the highest quality. They work on common platforms, use the latest software, and are networked as well as any university in the world. UITS provides uniform, integrated services throughout the university, and it is staffed by individuals with high levels of expertise. IU's life-cycle replacement program, rare among universities and a central part of the strategic plan, ensures that students, staff, and faculty have the computing power they need and minimizes maintenance costs. It allows digital library developers to assume current technology at the user's end, which enables the use of new and emerging technologies. Life-cycle replacement also extends to digital library-specific infrastructure (for example, servers, digitization equipment, and software) that is essential for creating sustainable persistent digital libraries. The strategic plan worked, in part, because it had funding attached to it. Funding provided a major incentive for buy-in and for our ability to realize the president's vision and to implement the plan successfully, but equally important was the commitment of the whole university community.

The IU library system and digital library program have capitalized on the strong, centralized IT structure that the IT strategic plan helped us develop. Activities such as archiving and system management—often the responsibility of the library automation specialists—are performed by UITS. The libraries have complete trust in the university's central IT infrastructure. Moreover, this centralization frees librarians, and particularly those in the Digital Library Program, to respond to critical changes taking place in teaching, learning, and research.

Development of digital resources, such as course management tools, emphasizes the need for a coordinated approach to networked information services. Many believe that integration is the most vital key to present success and dramatic growth in the future. Digital libraries will flourish in an integrated information landscape that maximizes resources, offers intersections that facilitate dialogue, deliberately promotes collaborative strategic planning, and enables more agile responsiveness to evolving trends in learning and research.

3. Forging Partnerships Is Essential to Realizing the Full Promise of Digital Library Development

The decentralized organization common to academic culture poses obstacles to the development of digital libraries as strategic aspects of the university enterprise. Suzanne Thorin and Daniel Greenstein, who have developed a collective biography of digital university libraries, note that one of the attributes that "distinguishes a digital library program is the library's relationship with surrounding academic departments and information services, such as computing and IT." They go on to say that "while it is not easily quantifiable, closeness may be measured by such factors as the facility and experience of collaboration between the library and these surrounding departments, and the extent to which strategic planning in one department includes representatives from and takes substantive account of other departments" (Greenstein and Thorin 2002).

Indiana University is among a fairly small group of libraries that have a strong relationship between their IT organization and their library—some others are the University of Southern California, Stanford, Columbia, and the University of Virginia. At many institutions, IT infrastructure is not centralized. Frequently, support and funding for libraries, including digital library development, are separate from support and funding for other IT activities in the university, thus creating silos of development and duplication of technology infrastructure. Such separation and duplication are especially problematic in this era of constrained resources. And they can slow the pace of change.

It is extremely difficult to build an integrated digital library program using existing resources and to fund program staffing and development on the margins of one's budget. Partnerships are essential in this regard. In fact, I would venture to say that such partnerships are no longer optional. They are critical. IU's Digital Library Program's joint funding arrangement maximizes dollars and reduces redundancy. We have jointly funded library appointments. The director of IU's Digital Library Program, the DLP's assistant director for technology, the library's director of IT—all are funded jointly by the two university units. This arrangement benefits the organizational structure by establishing formal lines of communication and ensuring that staff members work toward shared goals.

Partnerships outside of one's own university are also essential to digital library development. Only by working collaboratively, for example, can we find ways to share metadata across institutions and create search capabilities. The Open Archives Initiative (OAI) is one effort to address these challenges. A three-way partnership among Johns Hopkins University, Indiana University, and the UCLA Digital Library Program, the OAI-compliant Sheet Music Consortium aims to create a virtual catalog of sheet music in the United States. The Sheet Music Consortium is gathering data from large collections of American music to create a central searchable repository of descriptive metadata about the holdings in those collections and at the Library of Congress. While consortium member institutions catalog their sheet music in different ways, a large proportion of these materials have been digitized, thus providing users direct access to the music and, in some instances, to the covers and advertisements, which offer insight into the cultural context in which the songs were published. Partnerships such as these bring us a few steps closer to developing reliable principles for metadata and to creating transparent standards that will enable interinstitutional access to shared bodies of digitized and analog materials.

The evolving role of library information technology and the new emphasis on partnerships are leading to the creation of a digital repository accessible across all schools and campuses that would centralize the management, preservation, and distribution of currently localized digital collections and would address issues of licensed content and faculty research. As part of these explorations, IU is participating in FEDORA (Flexible and Extensive Digital Object and Repository Architecture), a project led by the University of Virginia Libraries and Cornell University's computer science department and designed to investigate issues raised by interinstitutional access to collaborative digital holdings. While undertaking these and other activities, we remain mindful that of equal importance to the development of centralized access and management of digital information is a shared vision of the library's digital future and the roles IT and other constituents can most strategically play in creating that future.

Research conducted as part of IU's Variations2 Digital Music Library project offers a case in point. Variations2 is a four-year project funded by an NSF grant that involves researchers and staff from UITS, the Digital Library Program, and IU's Schools of Music, Informatics, and Library and Information Sciences and our library. It is clearly in line with the PITAC recommendations to create several large-scale, federally funded digital library testbeds. Our testbeds are being implemented at IU's two research campuses in Bloomington and Indianapolis and at additional national and international partner or "satellite sites." The project's goals include providing users access to a collection of music in a range of styles and media formats and to developing multiple user applications on a single foundation of content and technology. The research and development layer focuses on usability that integrates user testing in design methodology, on the development and implementation of metadata guidelines for musical holdings, on intellectual property rights evaluations, and on network requirements for delivering high-fidelity, real-time audio and data for interactive music research and teaching applications.

4. The Role of Librarians and the University Library

Some years ago, with the rise of distance education and the emergence of institutions such as the University of Phoenix, it was predicted that the university campus would wither away as the educational content of degree programs was delivered on the learner's desktop. Along those lines, some may wonder whether the library as a physical place is becoming obsolete, or they may assume that, at the very least, its role needs to be reconceived in an era when so many reference and research materials are available to potential library users from their desktop computers.

With the creation of the groundbreaking Information Commons, Jerry Campbell at the USC both presented an answer to this question and established a model for others to follow. The University of Michigan's Media Union also illustrates how we can reconfigure the space of the physical library to continue its traditional function as a vital cultural environment, a social space that facilitates the exchange of ideas and information. We expect that IU Bloomington's new Information Commons, a highly integrated technology and information center, will be equally successful.

IU's Information Commons, which will open in fall 2003, grew out of complementary needs, and is the result of combining the complementary strengths of the library and IT organizations. Our technology organization recognized the increasing demand for more student technology centers, multimedia capability, and group workstation space, which are the responsibility of UITS. Space, particularly centralized space, is at a premium on campus. Simultaneously, the libraries felt the pressure of students' demand for 24/7 service and collaborative learning capabilities. An information commons, where students' technology and information needs can be met at one service point, provided a way to rethink the role of the undergraduate library. Students require group spaces with technology access. Faculty, likewise, require spaces for teaching and meeting. Both need workstations and technical support for the creation of multimedia presentations. The Information Commons will integrate technology with irreplaceable print collections and the resources of IT support staff with the expertise of library user and instructional services and reference staff. And it will serve as an intellectual gathering place, the sort of marketplace of ideas that remains a crucial element of any community of learning, even a twenty-first century one.

As many scholars have suggested, information overload is one of the greatest problems we will face in the future. The Internet is not a library, nor does it have the organized cataloging and commitment to preservation that make the library an accessible and imminently usable resource. More important, as James O'Donnell, author of *Avatars of the Word*, has pointed out, there is no filter. There is no sense that someone has surveyed the available resources and selected a set of materials that is both comprehensive and delimited. "On the Internet," notes O'Donnell, "you never know what you are missing."

How should librarians change to work more effectively in the digitized world? Large universities will have a continuing major role in providing access to huge print resources and in serving the faculty who use them. At the same time, they are building the future digital environment that will provide possibilities to integrate the library in vital new ways. Librarians have an opportunity to be much more than knowledge navigators. They have the opportunity to define the digital libraries of the future, but only if they are able to straddle the worlds of virtual and traditional collections.

In the digital age, libraries are no longer our primary storehouses of knowledge. More and more, the source of information is constantly at our fingertips. But like the Alexandrian library, the contemporary research library is more than ever before a vital hub of intellectual dialogue and discovery. It will continue to be the place where tributaries of knowledge converge and develop new currents of thought and creative activity.

Concluding Comments

Digital library capabilities are identified as necessary to the achievement of all the anticipated transformations of the information age outlined in the PITAC report and in the committee's earlier report to the president, *Information Technology Research: Investing in Our Future*. Many, if not all, of these transformations are central to the missions of universities. It is of the utmost importance for universities to direct their attention and resources to working—individually, in collaboration with one another, and in partnership with the government—to advance the state of knowledge and practice in digital libraries. In order to do so, universities must plan strategically to develop the IT infrastructure and services and the institutional arrangements that will enable digital libraries to realize their transformational potential in research and education and throughout society.

One of the more interesting digital projects currently under way serves as a good metaphor for my message today. The project, which is funded by the NSF, involves Stanford computer science engineers, archaeologists, and classics scholars in a partnership with the *Sovraintendenza* of the City of Rome. Their goal is to reconstruct the Severan Marble Plan, a highly detailed map that depicts the floor plan and every architectural feature of each building in ancient Rome. The map was carved on marble slabs that covered the entire back wall of the Roman Templum Pacis. Today, only 15 percent of this gargantuan city map exists, and it is broken into more than a thousand pieces. Classicists have tried for centuries to piece together the puzzle of the Severan Marble Plan. Now they are doing so by making a high-resolution digitized version of it available on the Web, so that a range of scholars can study the pieces. The research team is even developing a viewer that will allow members of the general public to match fragments and a slab map that reconstructs the known areas of the plan.

This is a wonderful example of how technology is making classical studies more accessible, but it is also a good analogy for our enterprise. As we survey a changing landscape, we, too, must try to fit the pieces together. In the same way that marble tablets gave way to other means of recording and disseminating information, paper and our treasured models of libraries as bricks-and-mortar repositories of knowledge will give way to new technologies, new paradigms, and new roles for librarians. Like the team of scholars reconstructing this map, we will collaborate to pool our knowledge and resources and to make strategic decisions.

The world is moving inexorably in the direction of library systems of collaboratively held collections that capitalize on integrated IT infrastructure and provide wide, yet organized, access to distributed information. It is up to the librarians at the nation's premiere research universities to lead the charge into this integrated information landscape and fully embrace the central role digital technology and materials will play in the library of the future. And it is up to university IT professionals to aid them in that effort through constantly deepening collaboration.

Acknowledgments

My most sincere thanks go to Susan Moke and Gerry Bernbom for all of their work on successive drafts of this paper. Thanks are also due to Karen Adams, Eric Bartheld, Kristine Brancolini, Jon Dunn, and SuzanneThorin for their valuable contributions to its preparation.

References

Greenstein, Daniel, and Suzanne Thorin. 2002. *The Digital Library: A Biography*. Washington, D.C.: Council on Library and Information Resources. Available at http://www.clir.org/pubs/abstract/pub109abst.html.

O'Donnell, James. 1998. *Avatars of the World: From Papyrus to Cyberspace*. Cambridge, Mass.: Harvard University Press.

President's Information Technology Advisory Committee. Report to the President. 2001. *Digital Libraries: Universal Access to Human Knowledge*. Panel on Digital Libraries. Technical Report. Available at http://www.ccic.gov/pubs/pitac/pitac-dl-9feb01.pdf.

President's Information Technology Advisory Committee. Report to the President. 1999. *Information Technology Research: Investing in Our Future*. Available at http://www.hpcc.gov/pitac/report/.

NEW MODELS FOR STEWARDSHIP

The Open Access Movement in Scholarly Communication

Michael Eisen

Scientific literature, the published record of the history of sciences, is one of humanity's greatest creations. I'm somewhat biased, but I think it is something we can all stand behind. The collection of ideas, methods, data, and discoveries—about our bodies and those of all the other animals in the world around us—especially as it pertains to human diseases, is an unbelievably rich and important creation of society over the last centuries.

The literature itself, one product of this endeavor, reflects the tremendous investment that society has made in raw dollar terms. Each year, probably $100 billion is devoted in one way or another to support scientific research, with the bulk of that going to medical research. It represents the life's labor of many of our brightest and most dedicated citizens, who have devoted their careers to trying to find ways of making our lives better, in both the material and intellectual sense, for people in this country and for the entire world.

The transformation that has occurred in the last 10 years, from a world in which we communicated primarily in print to one in which we communicate primarily digitally, has profound implications not only for how we access information, but also for how we use it. The potential to discover new ways of using the accumulated scientific knowledge is essentially infinite and has barely begun to be tapped.

A Wealth of Information Remains Out of Bounds for Most

The premise of this talk, which also motivates much of my own work, is that this potential we all dream about will remain largely unrealized as long as the scientific community persists in distributing information, and supporting that distribution, using practices that were developed for the print age and then just grafted wholesale onto the electronic age. I believe, and I think a growing number of scientists would agree, that it is both morally and practically absurd that we continue to grant the ownership of the scholarly product and the scientific product of the world to scientific publishers. I'll explain why I think this is true and tell you what some of us are doing to try to change that.

It is a travesty that this has occurred in science, because it is preventing people from doing interesting and new things in and with the literature. That is why I got involved. I studied genomes and am primarily a computational biologist. My main experimental tool is the computer, and I spend most of my days trying to recognize linkages between pieces of information that came either from experimental data or from the scientific literature. Six or seven years ago, large chunks of the scientific literature first started to become available in electronic form, and some of the most prominent journals started to be published electronically. I was a graduate student at the time, so I was somewhat naïve, but it seemed natural and obvious to me that we should be able to do something really interesting and useful with the text contained in all those papers, treating it not just as words on a piece of paper but rather as data.

I started to think about databases that would link the human genome sequence to the literature on the function of all of these genes and would allow people to navigate freely from the sequence to the literature. I began to imagine building these things, and I suddenly came upon a problem: it was impossible for me, as a research scientist, to actually do that. It was neither practically nor legally possible, and that seemed completely ridiculous to me. The scientific literature was produced by scientists, for people like me to use. The primary motivation for people who publish their work is that others will read it and use it. That is why I'm a scientist; that is why scientists are scientists. The fact that I could not do that just struck me as absurd.

Actually, this should be a scandal, both within the scientific community, where it is starting to get attention, and among the general public, who paid for this work in order to make it useful to them. It is silly that I cannot do this kind of research, and also ridiculous that people who have an interest in accessing this information but who do not have the good fortune of working for a major research university, or having access to a major research university library, cannot do this.

This is not just a theoretical idea. The chief executive officer of Elsevier is pretty happy to go around dismissing the idea that there is anybody in the world besides research scientists at Harvard and Stanford and Berkeley who actually want access to the scientific literature. But there are lots of other people, in this country and abroad, who have a real interest in accessing the scientific literature but cannot. Scientists at research universities in Zimbabwe do not have enough money to subscribe to even one or two journals, let alone all the scientific literature they are interested in. There are high school students and students and professors at small universities. My mother happens to be on the faculty at a small Catholic college in

Washington and cannot access any of the literature she is interested in using in her classes. So I have to surreptitiously send it to her on the side. (Sorry, I'm probably breaking a law by doing that.)

Even more important, this is an age in which we as citizens are being asked to take a much more active role in our own health care. When my doctor says to me, "I don't know, go study it yourself," I'm lucky. I can go to a medical library and read all this information. But say I'm a patient in a rural hospital who has been diagnosed with a relatively rare form of cancer that the federal government has been paying researchers to study and find ways of treating. Today, if I'm that patient, I cannot readily access the information that describes research done for my benefit and that would help me immediately and practically play a greater role in understanding my own health. There are myriad examples of people throughout the world who do not have the opportunity to access the literature that is available today, solely because of the way in which we have decided to structure the distribution of scientific information.

Those Who Do the Work Should Own the Literature

I have great faith in the ability of the scientific community, the library community, and the business community to discover new and interesting ways to use this literature. For my own purposes, I'm thinking about the creation of massive databases with literature on genome sequences. We build them in our lab from genome sequences and all sorts of other pieces of knowledge that we collect and disseminate. But as scientists, we are failing to include in that body of accessible information the most important element: the accumulated ideas, results, and conclusions of scientific research that are contained in the scientific literature.

Currently, scientific journals own the scientific literature. There is no other way to describe it. Journals get the copyright, which they wield as effectively as if they were the owners. I won't belabor the question of whether or not this is reasonable. We spend way too much of our time worrying about whether journals should own the literature. To me, it is obvious: they clearly should not.

Journals play an important role, a critical role, in bringing a scientific work to maturity. One writes a paper, submits it to a journal, and, after it has been peer reviewed, edited, and formatted, a different thing comes out the other end. But by no imaginable measure is the journal's contribution to this process comparable to the effort put into it by the scientists. Most work that comes out of my lab represents about two years of labor for a post doc, and maybe weeks or months of my time devoted to conducting the research, studying the results, and writing the paper. Every published scientific paper probably represents a quarter to half a million dollars of public investment.

If you compare that sustained effort of scientists around the world, plus the investment of public institutions, with the small role that journals have played in bringing scientific work to maturation, I think it is quite clear that the weight of the contribution belongs to the scientists and to the public, and not to the journals. You cannot come up with a system in which it makes sense, moral sense, that the journals should own the literature. The only questions I think worth asking are: Why is it that journals own the literature? Is there some practical alternative to the current system?

Legacy of Print Stifles Access and Cooperation

The answer to this is, of course, contained in the history of scientific publishing. I don't need to explain the business model of scientific publishing, or any publishing, that exists today. The journal largely takes on the burden of producing material and charges people who want to access the published information through subscriptions or through whatever licensing deal they have managed to convince libraries to agree to. This system evolved when we communicated on paper and the only effective way for scientists to communicate with their colleagues was to write a paper that was printed and shipped to libraries all over the world. In that world, most of the cost involved was in distributing printed copies of that manuscript. Since those costs scaled to the number of copies, it made some obvious economic sense for journals to charge on a per-copy basis if one bought a subscription.

This system was completely unfair in many ways. All these people who do not have access to the literature today did not have access to it in the print journal world, no matter how sensible and efficient that system was. But those restrictions were, at the time, logical and inevitable. There really was no better way to handle things. One can make a very strong and compelling case that the scientific journals have done a remarkably good and efficient job over the last century of disseminating scientific knowledge and that without the major boom in scientific journals after World War II a lot of the progress in science, especially in biological research, would not have occurred. We needed mechanisms to communicate our work to colleagues and researchers all over the world. I'm not here to criticize the journals for the job they have done; they truly have been quite useful to scientific society. And while there are many ways in which that system has been perverted—and some have started to charge more money than they should—that is not really our problem here today.

However, as soon as we started to communicate with one another electronically, all the premises of this business model completely evaporated. There are very few scientists today who get their literature primarily from the printed page. Most of us now download PDFs from a Web site and print out the document. We are reading printed copies, but the distribution itself is electronic, and when you have electronic distribution, you have completely different economics.

The costs involved in electronic scholarly publication are almost always in the preparation of the original, edited electronic document. These outlays are not trivial, but they remain as before the cost of managing peer review and hiring editors to oversee the process. But these are now the only costs involved. The cost of producing and distributing each additional copy is not zero, but it is very, very small, and there is almost no marginal cost every time someone wants to access or use a given copy of the literature.

Thus, the business model that developed in the print world, that of charging for each copy, has become economically irrational. It completely thwarts the best interests and goals of almost every stakeholder involved in the process other than the publisher. A lot of people try to make an analogy between scientific literature and Napster, or other methods of reproducing movies and music, where there is tension between the economic interests of the producer and those of the consumer. The producer clearly wants to get as much money and exposure as possible, while the consumer wants to get as much of the stuff he or she is interested in as cheaply as possible.

But in scientific publishing, the producers of the information and the consumers are the same people. I don't make any money from selling my work. All I care about is that people read my work and that they cite it. My interests and the interests of the institutions that funded my research, the interest of the public, and the interest of almost everybody except the scientific publishers, are best served in a world in which the scientific literature is completely open and freely available. We have allowed publishers to graft an economic model that evolved for print publication onto electronic publication, and this has happened with the complete complicity of scientists, the scientific community, and libraries. The fact that we have let this happen when it really did not have to is now the single biggest barrier to creating and developing new and innovative ways of using the scientific literature.

Toward a More Equitable and Rational Model

It is time for the scientific community, the public, and the educational institutions that support us to rethink this relationship we have with scientific publishers—to try to make sure that we develop an effective process for communicating with one another that does not unnecessarily compromise our interests solely for the sake of serving the financial goals of publishers.

The basic premise of an economically and functionally sustainable system is that costs really do exist in scientific publishing. Now that I myself am turning into a publisher, I recognize that these costs are legitimate and tangible. It takes money to manage peer review; it takes money to hire professional editors who can recognize quality research and help authors produce papers that are interesting and readable; it takes money to turn a manuscript into something that looks pretty on the page and is consistent; and it takes money to turn Word documents into XML that people can search and store in databases. These costs are not trivial; they are hundreds or thousands of dollars per article.

But rather than trying to recover those costs by subscription, which necessarily requires that access to the work be restricted, it seems that these costs should now be viewed as indispensable costs of actually doing the research. When I publish a paper, it is not an isolated event; it is the final step in a long and expensive process. It is the most public part of the research process, but still it is only a part. If scientists, and the academic and funding institutions that support our research, decided to view the costs I just listed as part of the research process, it would be possible to provide permanent, completely free, and open access to the finished product—not only to scientists, but also to anybody who wanted to read or use this literature.

We are reaching the stage where you can say there is a movement within the scientific community and the broader academic community to ensure that the open access way of making the product of scholarly communication available is the way of the future. There is some confusion about what is meant by this. Some argue that they already are providing free and open access to the literature, but in my opinion, this really is not so. By open access, I mean that the producers, the publishers of the literature and the information, do not put any restrictions, either practical or legal, on how this information can be used.

It has to be freely available. You have to be able to download it, and you have to be able to do anything with it, not just read and print it, but redistribute it, put it into a compendium or database, link sections of it to other pieces of information, do anything that is otherwise legal. Other than fraud, there is really nothing that one should not be able to do with the scientific and scholarly literature. The only thing that authors of this material ask, the only thing we really care about when you use our work, is that when you do, you say it was our work. The commodity we deal in is the commodity of citation and attribution, and it is the only restriction that legitimately can and should be placed on how scholarly literature is used.

There is no doubt that that if we adopted a system in which the costs of producing the literature were paid up front by the institutions funding the research process—the same institutions that fund, albeit more indirectly, the subscription costs for libraries—all of the important aspects of the current scholarly publication system would be maintained. But by removing a lot of economic inefficiencies, the system would actually be quite a bit cheaper. It would certainly be fairer and would serve best the interests of scientists in their roles as both authors and consumers, as well as the interests of the public and of all the institutions that supported our research.

Open Access Movement Finds Support—and Lingering Resistance

I think it is almost impossible to argue that this would not be a good thing, but it still has not happened. Why not? It might help here to talk a little bit about the history of this idea.

Seven years ago, when the idea first came to me and others with whom I ultimately worked, we thought that the logic of the new system was so patently beneficial for the scientific community that all we had to do was give people a way to communicate with each other. Physicists, as many of you know, had already been circulating their research through a preprint server, arXiv.org, a unified global raw database established in 1991 at Los Alamos and now based at Cornell. The physicists were happily communicating with each other, with no restrictions on how the information was to be used.

I figured that what works for physics should work for biomedical research. Fortunately, Harold Varmus was at the time director of the National Institutes of Health, and he was quite active in promoting the creation of a free full-text archive for biomedical literature, called PUBMED Central. When PUBMED Central came online in 1999, I expected most scientific journals, especially those published by scientific societies or those nominally part of the scholarly community, to see the obvious benefits of this system and to more or less immediately make their content available in PUBMED Central. At that time I was a post doc, no longer a graduate student but clearly still pretty naïve, because it did not happen: this system was created and almost nobody put their content into it. PUBMED Central, even though its great potential and usefulness should have been evident to all scientists, did not garner support from within either the scientific community or the publishing community.

So we tried something different. We tried to make it clear to publishers that the scientific community really wanted this, that this was something important to scientists, and that if journals would take the simple steps necessary to make their content available in this free and open manner, scientists would reward these journals with their support. We began to circulate an open letter and formed the organization Public Library of Science. Scientists signing the open letter pledged only to publish their work in, review and edit for, and personally subscribe to journals that took what we thought was a reasonable compromise position: they would make their content freely available on PUBMED Central or other suitable archives after six months. It may not be a perfect system, but we gave the journals six months to recover their costs through subscription charges, at the end of which they had to make their material freely available. That is, they got a lease rather than permanent ownership of the literature.

The open letter received a tremendous amount of support. It has now been signed by almost 35,000 scientists across the world. But the response of the publishing community to an effort by scientists to make the scientific literature more useful was largely silence and, in many other cases, overt hostility. Although a few did, most journals did not respond to the open letter in any consistent way, and so we have now moved on to another step.

"I Have Been Moved to Commit These Things to the Press"

Publishers are there, but we do not have to work with the established publishers. They are not the only way that scientists can communicate with each other. At the Public Library of Science, we started trying to do it ourselves. If the scientific publishers were not going to do what the scientific community wanted, we figured we would have to do it ourselves.

But clearly, we could not just do this ourselves; we needed some support. We spent a year and a half trying to garner support and find financial backing for this endeavor. Finally, in December 2002, we received a grant of about $9 million from the Gordon and Betty Moore Foundation in San Francisco to launch Scientific Publisher, devoted to providing immediate and free open access to the scientific literature, for any scientific work that a scientist wants to make available in this way. Harold Varmus, now head of Memorial Sloan-Kettering Cancer Center, is the head of the Public Library of Science.

Over the last six months, we have begun the process of launching a scientific publisher devoted to the principles I just outlined. To give you an idea of what we are doing, I want to quickly take a step back and go through the process we have been trying to understand. That is, why has this movement not been successful?

To do so, I want to quote from the introduction to the famous work, *On the Motion of the Heart and Blood in Animals*, by William Harvey, who worked out the circulation system in the human body. I am sure many of you have read the old introductions in some sixteenth and seventeenth-century books. They had a wonderful practice in which the author essentially had to apologize for writing the work. Harvey, trying not to take too much credit, has a great paragraph in which he explains why he decided to publish this work. I think it encapsulates all the reasons why scientists publish today:

> These views as usual, please some more, others less; some chid and calumniated me, and laid it to me as a crime that I had dared to depart from the precepts and opinions of all anatomists; others desired further explanations of the novelties, which they said were both worthy of consideration, and might perchance be found of signal use. At length, yielding to the requests of my friends, that all might be made participators in my labors, and partly moved by the envy of others, who, receiving my views with uncandid minds and understanding them indifferently, have essayed to traduce me publicly, I have been moved to commit these things to the press, in order that all may be enabled to form an opinion both of me and my labours.

Deconstructing this a little bit, Harvey wants to give further explanations of his work; he had been talking in public about some of this work, but he really needed to tell the whole story. This is one of the most important things we do in the published literature: give our complete stories. Harvey thought that other people would find use in this information. One of his prime motivations to publish the work was that others would use it, that others could be participants in his labors. I think it is important that through publishing, he did want not only to get the information out but also to give people an opportunity to judge his work.

I don't know whether Harvey was up for tenure or not, but it is certainly a big concern. I would say that it is probably the biggest challenge that the Public Library of Science faces, as we evolve from an advocacy group into a publisher. How do you accommodate the need for scientists not only to communicate their work but also to get the proper credit and acclaim for their best work?

Public Library of Science Launches an Alternative

We have now spent quite a lot of time thinking about why scientists have not embraced open access publishing, why biologists, for example, feel uncomfortable about putting their published papers directly into an archive. Why is it important for them to actually publish in a scientific journal? I think the answer is fairly clear. If a paper is self-posted, it has not gone through a process in which somebody, whether a couple of peer reviewers, an editor, or a publisher, has given a stamp of approval and stated that this work is not only worthy of being published but is of a certain level of quality.

Most of you are aware that there is a great hierarchy of scientific journals; for biologists, if you publish in *Science*, *Nature*, or *Cell*, it means you are at the top of your game. The scientific community does not just use these journals as filters to the literature, they are not only venues in which I know to look for the most interesting and best science. We have also essentially given *Science*, *Nature*, and *Cell* the gatekeeper role in deciding who gets hired at the lead universities, who gets tenure, who gets grants. If you have a series of publications in one of these journals, you have a real leg up in getting an excellent position and getting tenure. And if you do not have any publications in these journals, even if you have published work in another journal, no matter how good it is, people largely will not pay attention to it, and you will not get proper credit for having done excellent new research.

We decided that the most important thing the Public Library of Science could do as a publisher was to serve as an option that competed directly with *Science*, *Nature*, and *Cell* in providing the best scientific research. As of May 1, we are formally in existence, and *Public Library of Science Biology* will now try to tackle these journals head on. Our goal is to provide an open access journal, not just for downloading, but for any use. Every work we publish will be made freely available immediately and will be effectively in the public domain. The only difference between *Public Library of Science Biology* and *Science*, *Nature*, and *Cell* (other than that we will be a little bit better) lies in how we fund this endeavor.

We are asking authors to cover our costs up front, through charges of roughly $1,500 to $2,000 for each published work. I should add that our estimated costs are less than most authors already pay in page charges for many journals. Our production system is in place, we've hired editors from elite journals—in fact, we stole the editor-in-chief of *Cell* and she now works for us. Others have been knocking down our doors to come work for us, because I think everybody involved in scientific publishing who does not have a direct material stake in the outcome recognizes that this is the future.

So, *PLS Biology* exists. We have already received submissions, researchers want to send us their best work, and we have an editorial board that is better than that of other journals because scientists are strongly behind us. An alternative has been created, a journal that can and should—and will—be competitive with the best in the field. Others will no longer have any excuse for not adopting open access. It is now a test to see whether or not the scientific community and the institutions that support us are really behind this.

Libraries Are the Gateway to an Open Access Future

I have not yet said anything about libraries; to some extent, what we've been doing has been happening outside of the library system. Scientists spend less and less time in libraries, as I'm sure you know, because we are spending more and more time online. And most libraries have yet to become a central resource for scientists or a focal point for their electronic access to scientific literature and to scientific knowledge.

My own view of this has been that libraries have recently been thinking much too much about the cost of subscriptions and how to drive that down. I understand that libraries need to subscribe to the most recent literature and that the rising cost of subscriptions is causing a serious problem. But I have a proposition, and it is not that libraries should say to the established scientific publishers, "Try to get these costs down as low as possible, we are not going to subscribe to your high priced journals, we are now going to support journals that have lower subscription costs."

What I would like to hear libraries say is: "*Basta!*" Give *PLS Biology* journal some time, and then tell publishers, "No more subscriptions to scientific journals as of 2005. Libraries believe that the future of information, the future of scientific literature, is open access." It is the obvious choice for scientists, and if libraries were freed of the responsibility and burden of negotiating with publishers over subscription costs and licensing deals, it would be possible for libraries to actually do what I think that they can do best.

And as I've listened to others here, it sounds like what everybody wants to do is become the primary gateway, the electronic gateway, for scientists and scholars to access information and knowledge. Instead of being a place where one goes purely to access information, a library is the place to access information effectively, efficiently, and interestingly. If the scientific community, the library community, and the academic research community all banded together and simply said, "This is what is going to happen, publishers. We are no longer going to play your game. Do it the open access way or you are no longer involved," then everything would change overnight. Every publisher from *Proceedings of the National Academy of Sciences* to Elsevier would have no choice but to adopt this new, and I think much more efficient, publishing model.

Lessons in Deep Resource Sharing from the University of California Libraries

Daniel Greenstein

The research library's historic role is providing access to great collections of scholarly knowledge. To date, those great collections have been assembled in a single place, with a high level of professional service surrounding them, in support of research, teaching, and all sorts of civic and cultural engagements. The greatest challenge that research libraries face today is to fundamentally transform themselves so that they may continue to build and maintain those collections. I suggest that the traditional collection development model—one that assembles information resources and people in physical proximity to it in a single organization—is no longer a functional one. Instead, we are driven by the challenges we face to implement a new division of labor between organizationally distinctive, layered library services that work interdependently to provide individual users with the full suite of collections and services that they require.

Layering Library Services at the University of California

The story will be told with reference to the University of California (UC), where a layered library model is beginning to emerge. Before introducing the model itself, it is important to reflect a little on the context in which it is becoming realized. If it were a nation in its own right, the state of California would claim the fifth or sixth largest gross national product in the world. The state has two public university systems: the University of California and the California State University. The University of California has 10 campuses (the tenth, Merced, will begin enrolling students soon), nearly 200,000 student full-time equivalents, and about 5,000 faculty members. Its governance and funding are both highly decentralized.[1]

---

[1] The 10 campuses are Berkeley, Davis, Irvine, Los Angeles, Merced, Riverside, San Diego, San Francisco, Santa Barbara, and Santa Cruz.

UC also has 11 university libraries. Ten of these are located on the campuses (where they are in most cases themselves library systems), and one, the California Digital Library (CDL), is located at the Office of the President. Collectively, the libraries hold nearly 32 million volumes, and their combined annual budget includes some $240 million in state funding. Harvard libraries, by comparison, claim some 14 million volumes. In maintaining the breadth and depth of their collections, UC libraries, like other great research libraries, are hard pressed to keep up with the escalating costs of scholarly publications. These costs have risen more rapidly than library budgets in the past several years. Figure 1 shows the extent of the challenge. It compares a price index calculated for scholarly journals with the consumer price and higher education price indices, respectively, and demonstrates that libraries—in good years as well as in bad—cannot keep up with the annual 6–12 percent price increases in scholarly journal subscription costs.

Figure 2 shows the same problem in a slightly different way. It charts the annual increase in the number of volumes published worldwide with the declining purchasing power, in volumes, of the state funding that libraries receive for monograph purchases.[2]

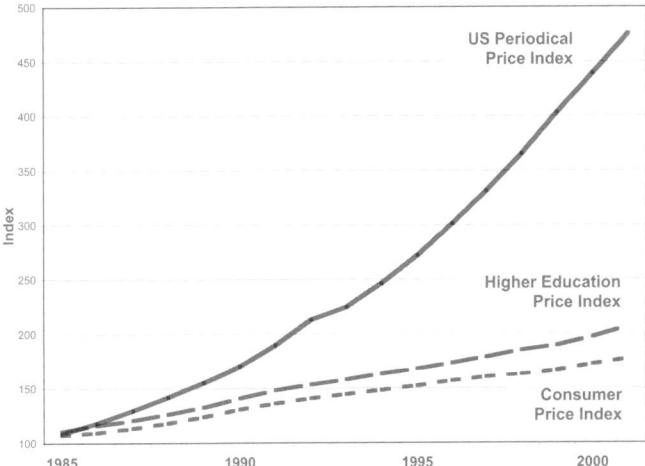

Fig. 1. Periodical price increases in comparison with common inflation indexes, 1985–2000

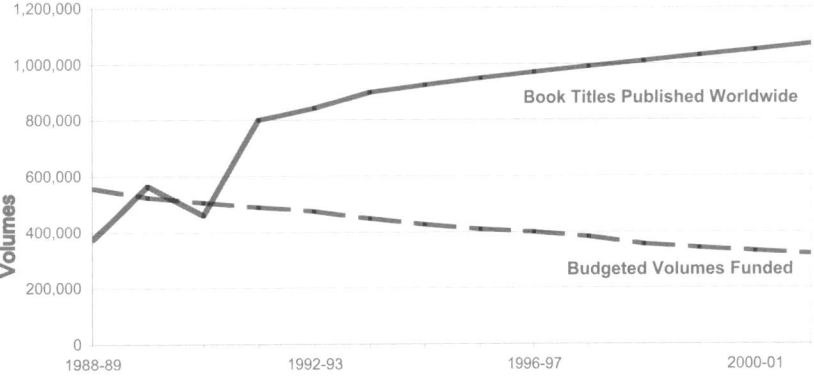

Fig. 2. Growth in publishing and decline in library buying power, 1988–2001

---

[2] U.S. libraries manage somehow to acquire some 650,000 books annually using endowment and other funding. Even at that rate, they are unable to keep pace with the rate of publication.

This inflation in both the volume and the cost of scholarly publications has forced the UC libraries to seek new ways of maintaining their historic collecting roles. In particular, they have invested collectively in services that all require but that none can afford independently. Looking briefly at a number of these services, we will see a layered library service model beginning to emerge, one in which campus libraries build upon a range of common or utility services in order to better meet the very distinctive local needs of their own faculty, students, and civic constituencies.

Regional Libraries, a Union Catalog, and a Digital Collection

The regional library facilities (compact print storage facilities of which UC has two, in the north and the south) were an early, perhaps the first, UC experiment with a new library service model. These facilities that are paid for centrally and managed (by Berkeley in the north and UCLA in the south) for the use of the libraries generally, free up scarce shelving space that is available in campus libraries, thereby enabling them to keep locally maintained collections current.

A second utility is a union catalog, Melvyl®, which makes information available to any user, anywhere in the system—anywhere in the world, in fact—about the UC libraries' collective holdings. By combining Melvyl with an online patron initiated interlibrary loan service (a further utility), the UC libraries give their users access to more than 32 million volumes as if they formed part of a virtual uniform library. Figure 3 shows the results of an online search conducted using Melvyl. A publication called *Adaptive Instructional Systems* is not widely held by the UC libraries. So a user at Riverside who is interested in the title clicks the Request button, and the volume is delivered within 24 to 48 hours.

Another utility, of more recent origin, is a collection of digital materials that the libraries agree to license or purchase together. The collection is one of the largest made available digitally by a research library and at present includes more than 8,000 journal titles, 250 reference and other databases, all books printed in English before 1800, 200,000 digital images of works of art and architecture, and 4,500 social scientific and government statistical databases. Nothing in this collection is acquired that is not agreed to and paid for by every library.[3] The rationale for the shared digital collection's development is simple. Digital information doesn't need to live anywhere in particular and can be accessed from anywhere over the network. Rather than acquiring highly redundant local digital collections, the UC libraries began in 1997 to acquire some digital materials together—not as a buying club, but as a single corporate entity. By sharing in the development of digital collections, the UC libraries can effectively share in a variety of essential tasks, including identification, review,

---

[3] Payments are made according to a prorated formula that is worked out and agreed to by the campus libraries.

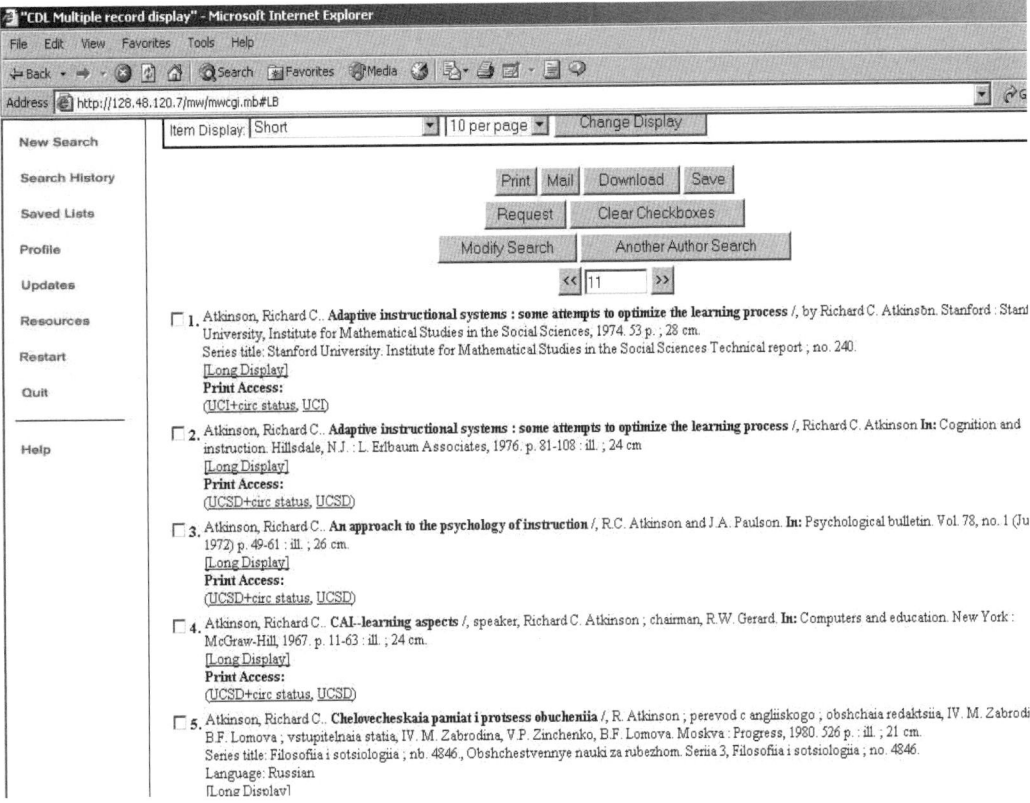

Fig. 3. Melvyl and patron-initiated request

vendor negotiation, content acquisitions, and acquisitions processing. They also exercise and enhance their buying power acting as the University of California libraries.

A next step, a very new one for the UC libraries, is to think about extending the shared collection from digital to printed materials. The UC libraries are, for example, building shared collections of printed journals that exist in digital formats and exploring the development of shared collections of federal and state government documents. The rationale for print is as it is for digital:

- enhancing collections and services that each UC campus library makes available to its faculty and students;
- expanding the breadth and depth of collections available system-wide to support the university's distinguished teaching and research programs;
- reducing unnecessary duplication of campus holdings; and
- saving substantially in cost and effort.

Planning for the shared print collection has been a revealing process and has forced us to ask hard but essential questions. Of the materials on our libraries' shelves, which of them do we need to continue holding redundantly? Are there economies to be had through some coordination? How can shared print holdings be collaboratively governed?[4]

---

[4] These themes are more fully developed in Daniel Greenstein, "Library Stewardship in a Networked Age: The Compelling Logic of Shared Collections," in *Redefining Preservation in the Twenty-first Century*, edited by Abby Smith. Forthcoming.

We are starting with print materials where cooperative collection development makes obvious sense, notably with new journals (e.g., as published by Elsevier and the Association for Computing Machinery [ACM]) where a single print edition is supplied "free" to the UC libraries in respect of their systemwide electronic site license. In these economic times, when libraries are beginning to cancel print subscriptions where electronic versions exist, we are also expecting this kind of shared collection to ensure that print editions aren't knowingly or willingly lost to the system. We are also thinking retrospectively about focusing not only on journals that are available online but also on federal and state government publications. In an interesting hallway discussion recently, two of our university librarians found themselves wondering whether and to what extent libraries should share in the cost of "core" materials, leaving campus libraries to enhance, maintain, and assert their distinctiveness by investing in distinctive local collections.

The shared print collection is yet another example of a utility set of services. It enables campus libraries to provide a higher level of collection and service support for research and teaching on their campuses and for the various public communities they serve.

The layering model is also evident in a range of technology applications that are supplied by the California Digital Library in close cooperation with the campus libraries. One example is a reference linking service that is demonstrated in figures 4-7. In figure 4 a user is searching in OVID's *Current Contents*—an abstract and indexing database—for journal articles on strokes. Having located a promising reference to *Anatomy of Stroke, Part I*, she wants to see the full text of the article. Clicking on the reference, she does (figure 5). If the user then sees a footnote or reference to something that he or she also wishes to read, clicking on that reference will pull up the full text of that article (figures 6-7). But links from *Current Contents* will not always lead to the full text of an article. In fact, the links can be made only if the article text is available under license at UC. In some instances, only the print edition is available, in which case the user may end up back at Melvyl, having to issue a request for an interlibrary loan.

This linking utility is a particularly interesting model of a layered service. The CDL hosts technology that enables this kind of linking and uses that technology to ensure that it applies wherever possible to the electronic content that makes up the shared digital collection. But the shared digital collection does not constitute the sum total of electronic materials to which UC faculty and students have access. Campus libraries acting individually and in small groups also license or purchase electronic information over and above that which is available in the shared collection. To ensure that campuses can integrate the unique electronic materials that they hold, the CDL makes the linking technology that they maintain available to the campus libraries; these libraries in turn configure the linking service to include locally held online materials.

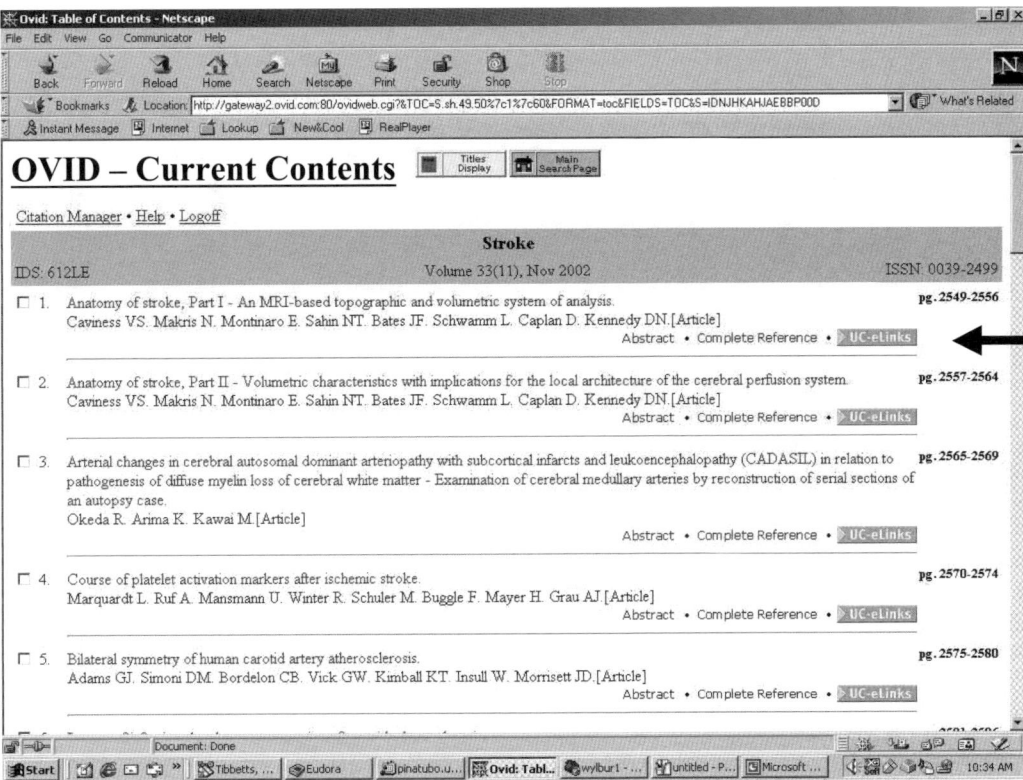

Fig. 4. Reference linking from *Current Contents*

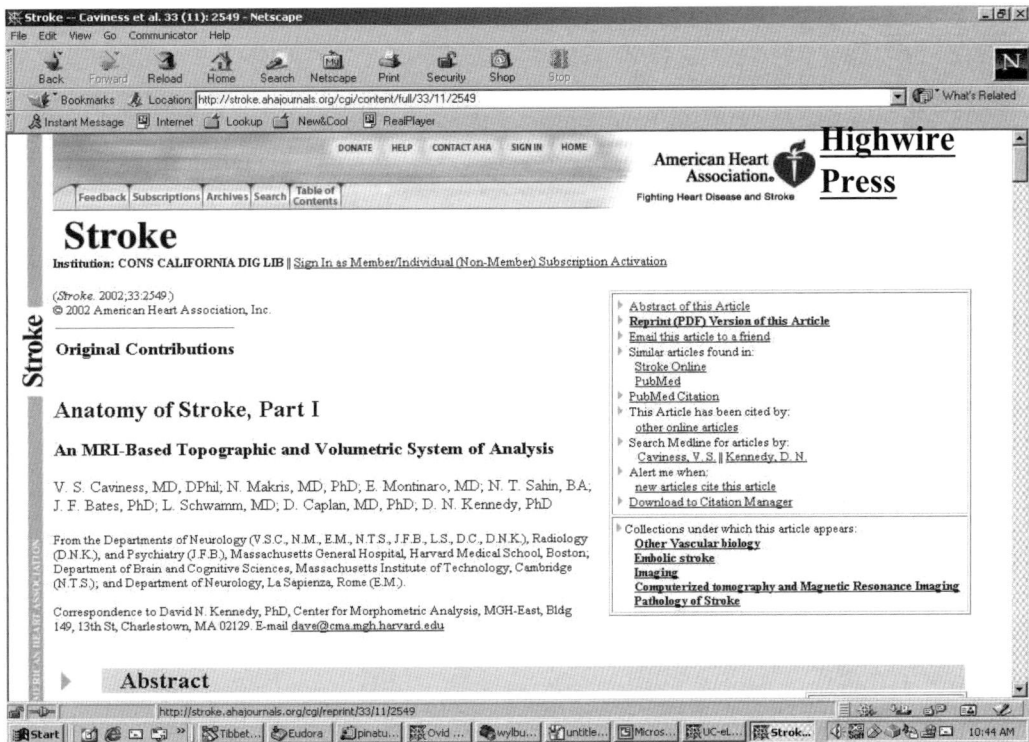

Fig. 5. Link found in *Stroke*

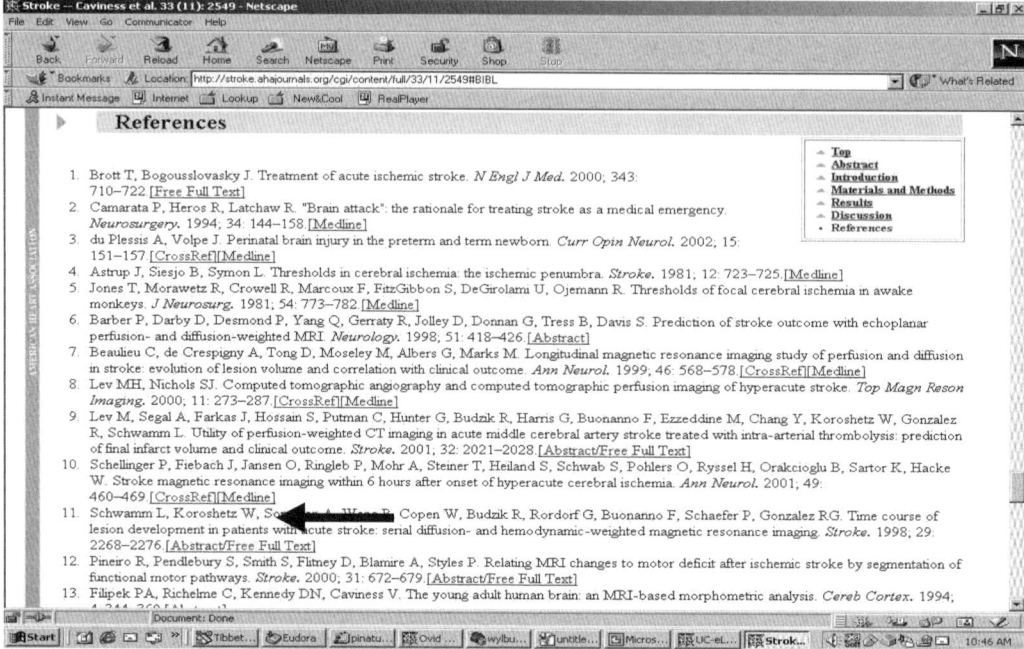

Fig. 6. Reference linking from a footnote in the article in *Stroke*

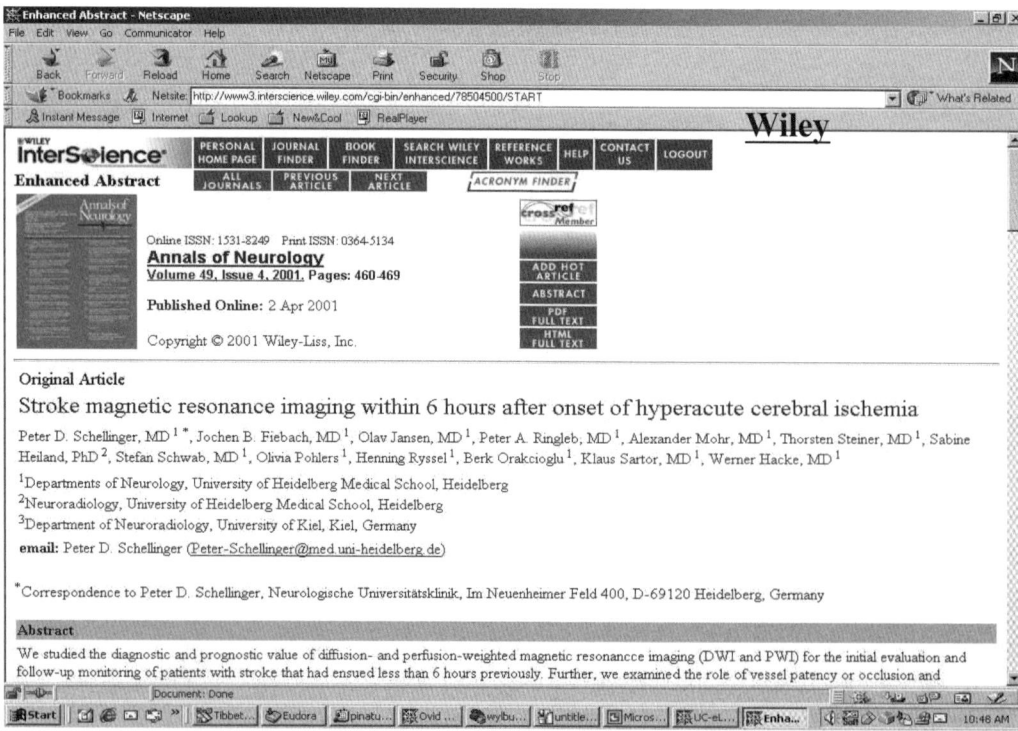

Fig. 7. Link found in the *Annals of Neurology*

A Union Catalog of Finding Aids

A further example of a layered service is the Online Archive of California (OAC), a union catalog of some 7,000 finding aids that have been developed for library special collections and archives on UC campuses and more generally around the state. Bound up within the OAC are perhaps two enabling utilities. A technology infrastructure enables integration of disparate finding aids. Perhaps more interesting, the OAC as a project provided the guidelines, and in some cases the motivation, to campus and other collections to produce online finding aids in a format that could be integrated. A new service that integrates access to digital image surrogates for works of art and architecture may have a similar effect and help UC's libraries and museums make hundreds of thousands of digital images available to the widest possible community. As with other utilities, this one is designed to enhance the local services that campus libraries can make available to their users. In this vein, we are exploring the development of tools that will enable libraries to configure the service to meet local users' specific needs, for example, by adding local images to the collection, by integrating the image collection with other local holdings, and by building interfaces that ensure the image service as a whole integrates with local course management systems.

What Makes the Layered Service Model a Challenge

This brief review of the layered services that are available within UC suggests that there is nothing at all new about the service model. The great public utilities (electricity, gas, even water) have been provided on a similar model since the late nineteenth century. What is new is the application to library services of this layered model. Also new are the weaknesses in the digital library that the model's development at UC has revealed, and it is to these challenges that the paper turns.

Figure 8 depicts schematically and somewhat abstractly the current digital library service model. It shows star shapes toward the top of the picture to represent library Web sites where users come to find a host of materials (online public access catalogs, online journals, online databases, etc.). Libraries construct the Web sites for their users. They make reference to a wide variety of information resources represented as oval shapes toward the bottom of the picture. These information resources may include

- catalogs of materials that are available locally in print and other analog formats (e.g., through online public access catalogs and finding aids);
- online materials that are available to local users under licenses and that may be managed by third parties (e.g., online journals and reference databases); and
- freely accessible Internet-based materials that are accessible through the library Web site and may be hosted anywhere in the world.

Because information resources are built differently in a variety

Fig. 8. The current digital library service model

of places, by a variety of people, and to serve a variety of means, the library has to work quite hard and often in very proprietary, ad hoc ways (demonstrated by differently depicted arrows) to include them in its Web site. The model is enormously ineffective and inefficient. Take the library's integration into its Web site of online journal content as an example. Operating at the content layer (represented by ovals), journal publishers have produced a host of different products, each of them aggregating or assembling in one place a particular collection of journals. Although the aggregations tend to focus in particular subject areas and can be quite large, they are only a very partial representation of the available journal content. Rather than look exclusively at one publisher's collection of scientific journals, for example, the library user wants to look across a host of publishers' science offerings. To support this research, the library is forced to combine, in a single Web site, a wide variety of journal collections, linking collections wherever possible by using the reference-linking technology discussed above. In effect, the library spends considerable energy in disaggregating the publisher aggregations so the journal content they contain can be more useful. Further, the library is charged doubly for its inconvenience. It pays a premium in subscription costs for the so-called value-added services that publishers claim they add by aggregating content. It then pays again to support the reference-linking technologies that allow it to unbundle aggregations so that the materials become more useful.

Many journal publishers have recognized the burden that the model imposes and have organized themselves through CrossRef so that they universally support network protocols that enable cross-collection linking. Unfortunately, the hard lessons learned are apparently not having any influence over those monograph publishers who are beginning to make some of their backlists available online.

Once again, we see the publishers' insistence on aggregating online content in ways that make little sense to library users, who typically want unfettered access to a range of information products. Indeed, the model emerging with electronic monographs may prove to be more flawed than that which is only now being transformed in the journal market. At least the journal publishers went out of their way to aggregate content by discipline, including in any one aggregation the journals of many different academic societies and, sometimes, publishers. With online monograph collections, the organizing principle that is most commonly in evidence seems to be by publisher (and perhaps, within publisher, by subject).

Commercial electronic publishers are not the only or even the worst offenders. Libraries that produce their own digital collections (for example, by scanning selected special collections) do so in a way that makes it extremely difficult for others to federate and integrate those collections with one another and with the more foundational holdings of printed and electronic monograph and journals. Have we, too, developed content that is so distinctive and ad hoc in its local orientation that it forces others who want to use it to go through the same unbundling process that commercial journal and monograph publishers force upon us?

A more rational digital library model is depicted in figure 9. The model proposes that we (publishers, libraries, anyone who builds digital information content) develop digital content and distribute it in open repositories. The repositories are "open," not because they are freely accessible (the model doesn't prejudice business decisions) but because the digital objects they contain (whether they are encoded texts, digital images, digital sound or film, statistical databases, or geospatial information systems) can be accessed, transformed, combined, and recombined with objects drawn from other collections by bona fide users according to their needs and interests. The model does not constrain the journal or book publishers, or even the digital

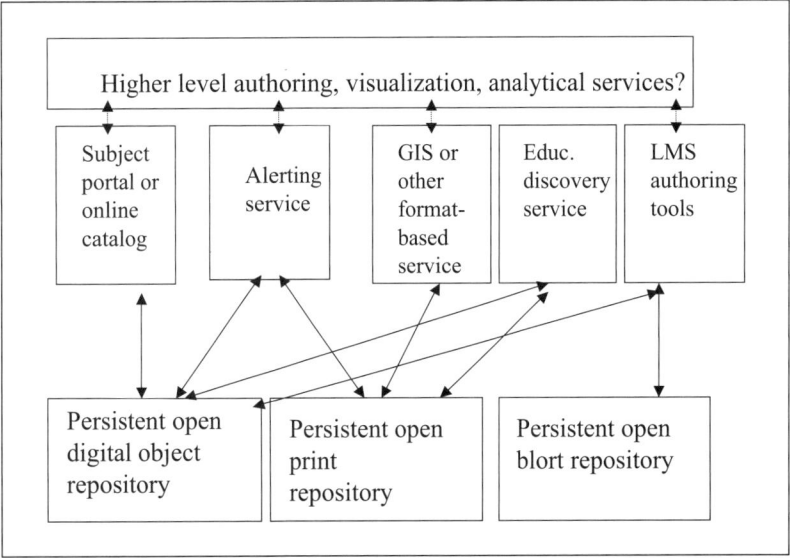

Fig. 9. A layered approach

libraries, from aggregating content in their own unique ways or distributing it with their own look, feel, brand, and functionality. They will and they must continue to build "higher-level" end-user services based on the content they supply. The model simply suggests that perhaps others will want to develop different higher-level services supporting needs and uses that the content owners cannot envisage. The model also forces us to think creatively about what kind of higher-level services might materialize if digital information content is available in open repositories. At present, the only higher-level services that we know are union catalogs (which integrate access to information about holdings of different online information resources) and, more recently, linking services as discussed above. Although there is a great deal more to do before we can claim to have perfected these kinds of services, we might still want to ask whether there are others that we have not yet thought of.

What about alerting services, which indicate to users that something in their field of study has just become available from one or other source? Or format-based services that integrate access to and encourage use of online maps or space data? What about authoring tools that allow users to weave an interpretive web around digital objects (online journals, encoded books, manuscript images, databases) that are found in a variety of different open repositories and to present the interpretive web as an interactive lesson in support of online learning? Can we surface online library information in a manner that allows it to be integrated selectively into online learning materials, whether the materials are developed in Blackboard, WebCT, or some proprietary system? The answer, sadly, is no. At the University of California, this translates financially as follows: the $240-million annual investment that UC makes in its libraries is not available to the $170-million investment that it makes in instructional technologies. And UC is by no means unique in this.

There are other challenges. Even if we do adopt a layered model and put at its foundation a range of open digital object repositories, we are uncertain about how best to manage our digital content. What we do currently is perhaps best exemplified with reference to the many lives of a digital image surrogate for a work of art. Let's say that a library wishes to develop an online finding aid to assist users interested in accessing its slide library. That library might include for every record in the catalog a thumbnail of the image of the slide in question. The thumbnail image is produced, included in a catalog record, bundled into a database management system that is useful for cataloging, and made accessible through a range of search-and-retrieval functions that are appropriate to a catalog. If the same library wants to include images that are available from the slide library in, say, an online collection of works by German expressionists, it will create an altogether different image (probably at higher resolution), bundle it along with some descriptive data in an altogether different content management system (e.g., as appropriate to an online image service), and make it available through a variety of search, retrieval, slide-table, and other functions as specifically appropriate to such a service. Then let's assume that a teacher who is presenting a class on a particular German expressionist wants to create some online learning materials utilizing some of the same digital images that are now available both in the catalog and in the image service. She will in this case have to reproduce the digital image and include it along with any descriptive information in an entirely separate content management system, this one providing the functionality as appropriate to online learning materials.

The model, depicted in figure 10, relies upon proliferation of parallel and independent services, each with its own data ingest, data management, and data delivery schemes. It doesn't scale. Every time the library wants to use a single digital object (whether an image, a graph, a map, or a text) in a new way, it is almost forced to build another vertical and independent silo of infrastructure and technology around it. That's pretty silly. In the more rational model depicted in figure 11, the library's digital images are managed in a single consistent format as part of one or several open image repositories that are constructed in a way that supports very different users of selected digital images. This is where we think we are going at UC, as at many other research libraries, and we are going in this direction because the parallel model (figure 10) is so uneconomical.

Conclusion

The layered service model also forces us to think differently about organizational issues. In it, we give up on any understanding that the content producer (the entity responsible for the open digital object repository) can know all the various ways in which the digital objects they produce will ultimately be presented and used. Abstractly, the repository cannot predict the range, complexity, or functionality of the higher-level services that are built on top of it. The question

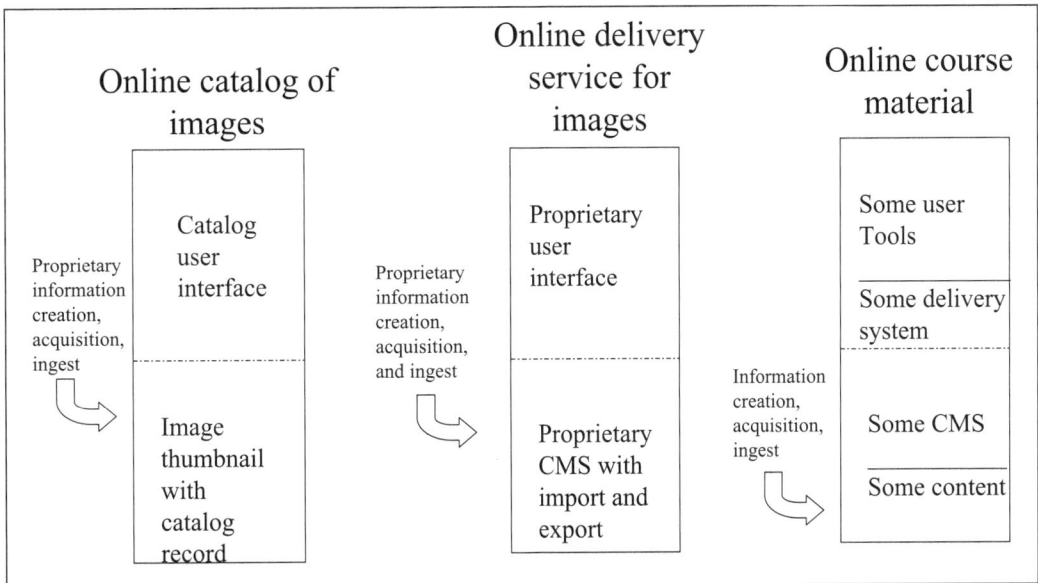

Fig. 10. Content management: the parallel service model

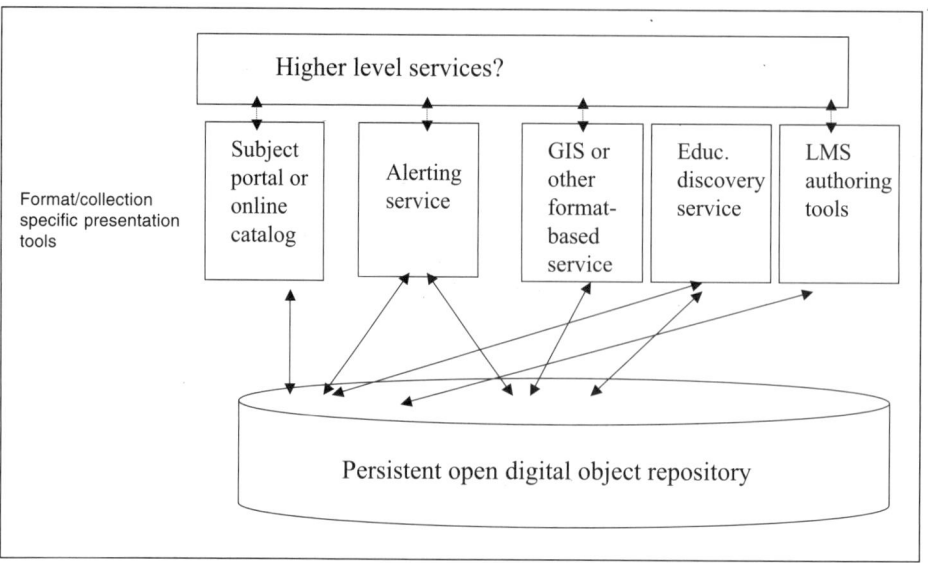

Fig. 11. Content management: a layered model

then becomes how to build a repository so that it can support a virtually infinite array of unknown higher-level services. Any answer to this question will undoubtedly be technical, but it will necessarily include organizational and political aspects as well. In a layered model, the success of those building open digital object repositories will be tied directly to the success and visibility of those building higher-level services based upon them. The promise that the model holds for libraries is compelling.

Today, we heard talks by people from public, national, and research libraries. Many of us have talked about the wonderful independent services we have created, services that array themselves in parallel to one another and comport themselves according to some organizational independence. Perhaps in two or three years we will return and speak in a different way. Then, perhaps, public librarians will speak eloquently about the services they have built for a local community on top of the collections offered up by research and national libraries. And the research librarians might in turn speak with passion about how they are delivering their collections through services developed by civic libraries and by schools—services that are tailored to specific user communities and user needs. Is it possible that a layered service model permits an organizational division of labor through which a variety of organizational entities, each playing different functional roles, are equally empowered?